Becoming a
Values-Based
Leader

Becoming a Values-Based Leader

Homer H. Johnson

Loyola University Chicago

INFORMATION AGE PUBLISHING, INC.
Charlotte, NC • www.infoagepub.com

Library of Congress Cataloging-in-Publication Data

Johnson, Homer H.
 Becoming a values-based leader / Homer H. Johnson.
   p. cm.
 ISBN 978-1-61735-789-3 (pbk.) – ISBN 978-1-61735-790-9 (hardcover) –
ISBN 978-1-61735-791-6 (ebook)
 1. Leadership. 2. Values–Psychological aspects. I. Title.
 HD57.7.J6436 2012
 658.4'092–dc23

                                                     2012003211

Printed in the United States of America

Contents

Foreword

It is impossible to be a leader without values. Everyone has them. Values drive human behavior, defining those who possess them, for better or worse. Churchill and Gandhi had them, and so did Hitler and Stalin. In this book, Homer Johnson explains how to become a more effective values-driven leader, for better. He shares his thoughts and feelings within a business narrative because he wants his reader to accompany the central character, Dave Hanson, on a journey of personal discovery. As the story begins, the fictional CEO of MMS (a fast-moving medical supply company) is worn-out, indeed burned-out, and tempted to quit until talked out of it by a friend and mentor, Charlie Schaefer.

Others will have their own reasons for praising this book. Here are two of mine. First, Johnson tells a great story. The characters are memorable, the dialogue rings true, the plot developments are plausible, and the eventual resolution of conflicts seems natural. The credibility factor is especially strong.

The advice Dave receives from Charlie is best revealed within the lively narrative. However, I will note what Yogi Bera once acknowledged, "We have met the enemy and he is us." To paraphrase Pogo, as Dave eventually learns, "We have what we need to defeat the enemy and he is us."

I also appreciate the substance of the material that provides a framework for Johnson's story. Many (most?) business narratives seem flimsy. Rather than rely on disappearing cheese or melting icebergs, Johnson an-

Becoming a Values-Based Leader, pages vii–viii
Copyright © 2012 by Information Age Publishing
All rights of reproduction in any form reserved.

chors his insights within the real world, in a human context. We have all met people like Dave and Charlie. Many of us have also experienced a "crucible" in our career or personal life.

Given the current economy especially, many of us can identify with Dave's fears and frustrations. The power, impact, and value of this book will depend almost entirely on the nature and extent of each reader's interaction with the material that Johnson provides.

Some books resemble magic carpets as they transport readers to the plains of Troy or to fantasy worlds inhabited by Red Queens and Mad Hatters. Homer Johnson's book enables readers to accompany Dave on his journey but, and more importantly, he urges them and will enable them to complete their own journey of discovery or rediscovery. I join with him in wishing each reader "bon voyage!"

––––––––––––––

Bob Morris has reviewed more than 1,500 business books for Amazon's U.S., UK, and Canadian websites. Feedback from those who have read his reviews currently rank him #13 among more than four million reviewers. You are welcome to check out his website, http://bobmorris.biz/.

Preface

The basic premise of this book is that effective leaders—indeed, people who will make a significant impact in this world—are people with a strong sense of purpose, and strong positive values that guide their actions and behavior. This is the definition of values-based leadership.

There are plenty of real-world examples of values-based leaders. Reverend Martin Luther King is one of my favorites. Here was a person who was constantly under fire. He was repeatedly threatened; he was physically assaulted; his house was bombed; he was arrested numerous times; and in the end, he was assassinated. But through all of this he never wavered in his commitment to his purpose and values. It was this commitment that was the basis for his ability to lead the struggle for civil rights.

In the business area, Sam Walton, the founder of Wal-Mart, is another one of my favorites. A man with a clear sense of purpose and mission, and strong personal values, he not only built America's largest company, but inspired many employees and others along the way.

The list could go on indefinitely. I often ask students to pick a leader that they think is values-based, and tell me a story about the person's purpose and values. The people they pick are from all areas of life—some people pick religious leaders, such as Pope John XXIII, or Dietrich Bonhoeffer, the Lutheran minister who defied Hitler; political leaders such as Abraham Lincoln or Hillary Clinton; business leaders such as Warren Buffett, CEO of Berkshire Hathaway, or Bob McDonald, CEO of Procter & Gamble; or

Becoming a Values-Based Leader, pages ix–xii
Copyright © 2012 by Information Age Publishing
All rights of reproduction in any form reserved.

sports leaders, such as Coach K from Duke, or C. Vivian Stringer, the Rutgers championship coach.

Still others cite one of their high school principals, their manager at work, the minister of the church they attend, or their college athletic coach. This latter list illustrates one of the premises of values-based leadership, which is that the leaders we interact with everyday are the core of a good society. It is the people who are out in the trenches, and who lead with purpose and values, that make this a better world.

Following from the discussion above, I make six assumptions regarding values-based leadership:

1. It is those people who have a strong personal values base who have made and will make important (positive) contributions to their families, organizations, and the world.
2. While the literature focuses on heroic leaders, the Martin Luther Kings and the Abraham Lincolns of the world, it is people showing leadership in the everyday tasks of everyday life that will, in the long run, make for a better organization or a better world. While not diminishing the contributions of our heroes, most people are not focused on saving the world, but rather they are focused on living their lives and doing their jobs. It is these "quiet leaders" who create better places for us to live and work.
3. Values and leadership come from inside the individual. Thus, if you want to make an impact, it is critical that you understand who you are and what you believe.
4. Values-based leadership includes both process and outcomes. An elementary school teacher should not only treat each student with dignity, but also has the responsibility for making sure that students are learning in accordance with standards and potential.
5. Organizations can and do espouse values. Values become the basis for how organizations operate and are the foundation of their culture. The values are expressed in the policies and procedures, in leadership behavior, and a variety of little ways. Strong values organizations are more successful in the long term than are weak values organizations.
6. Values-based leaders create values-based organizations, groups, teams, families, and communities. By the standards they set, the decisions they make, the behaviors they exhibit, and the philosophy they espouse, values-based leaders have a significant influence on the behaviors of others and the workings of organizations.

This is not to say that having a purpose and set of values to guide your life will solve all of your leadership problems. Sometimes your values don't quite fit the situation. Or more often, your personal values may conflict with one another. Consider the situation in which your best friend asks you to recommend him for a promotion but you really think he would be a disaster. How do you balance friendship to your friend (who is a little sensitive about what people think of him), with your value of honesty? Not an easy choice for most people.

Or, what happens if your values are challenged? I often have students read Reverend Martin Luther King's "Letter from Birmingham Jail," which is easily accessed through Google. King was strongly criticized by the clergymen in Alabama for his nonviolent protests in Birmingham on behalf of the garbage handlers. It is one thing to be criticized by the Klu Klux Klan, but criticism from your fellow clergy really needs to be taken a bit more seriously. What I like about the letter, which he wrote while incarcerated in the Birmingham Jail, is that it outlines his struggles with the criticism. Were his actions correct and justifiable, given his values and the situation in Birmingham? Or were his critics correct? Actually, it is probably helpful to have our values challenged occasionally. It forces us to reflect on who we are and what we stand for.

This all begs the question as to how one becomes a values-based leader. That is what this book is all about. Using a story format, the book tells the story of Dave, the CEO of MMS, a fast-moving medical supply company, who has "burned out" as a leader. Dave's proposed solution is to quit his present job and look for work at another company. However, an old friend and mentor convinces him that the problem is not with the job he is in, but rather it is with himself, Dave, and recommends an executive coach. By working with the coach, Dave goes through a series of exercises by which he rediscovers his purpose and values, and, in turn, renews his enthusiasm and effectiveness as a leader.

The format allows the reader to go through the same step-by-step process as the central figure of the story. By understanding how Dave went through the process of discovering or rediscovering his purpose and values, and by also engaging in the same process, the reader can hopefully rediscover his or her own purpose and values, and move toward becoming a values-based leader. I wish you the best of success in your journey.

Finally, many thanks to the hundreds of undergraduate and graduate students who have gone through this process, and, I hope, are now leading families and organizations from a values base. And a special thanks to two values-based leaders whose support was critical. First, to my "boss," Father

Mike Garanzini, SJ, the President of Loyola University Chicago, who exemplifies how values-based leaders lead and how they create highly successful organizations. And secondly, to Bob Morris, who wrote the Foreword to this book. Bob probably has critically reviewed more books on leadership than anyone else on this earth, and his endorsement of this book is very important to me. Thank you both.

1

Denver Airport

"I could have predicted this," muttered Dave Hanson rather angrily, as he looked at the departure board at the Denver airport. "This week has been a string of disasters, so why not end the week with one?"

The posting on the board stated that his 3:45 p.m. flight out of Denver had been delayed because of inclement weather over Denver. The probable take off time was now scheduled for 5:45 p.m., assuming, that is, that the weather clears. Nothing was flying out of Denver so it didn't make any sense to try to find another carrier that had a flight out before 5:45.

Dave mentally went over the disasters of the week. Monday started with a major product recall that could cost the company millions. On Tuesday one of his top manufacturing gurus gave him two weeks' notice. He said he was leaving—said that Dave wasn't listening to him. On Wednesday a major customer decided to change to another supplier. Thursday he met with the outside accountants who wanted to restate the first quarter earnings—there was a reporting error they picked up in an audit. And today, Friday, is "ethics day," he thought rather cynically.

Becoming a Values-Based Leader, pages 1–6
Copyright © 2012 by Information Age Publishing
1

This was Dave's third year as the CEO of MMS, an innovative start-up company that manufactures and distributes medical supplies, mainly to the hospital and rehab center market. The company strategy was to link with the hospitals they served through their mutual computer systems, such that the hospital would always be fully stocked with the supplies they needed. Thus, there was no need for the hospital to be continually ordering supplies.

Moreover, MMS's research group was continuously innovating in the hospital equipment area and offered to the hospitals "the latest innovations in the hospital area." Most of their manufacturing was in the Far East and with independent contractors; however, they had an active manufacturing group to assist the independent contractors with manufacturing design and quality control. All in all, MMS was considered an aggressive and innovative company that had been capturing market share in the U.S. market and who had ambitious plans to expand to other countries.

Dave appeared ideal for the CEO position at MMS. With a degree in marketing, Dave's first real job was with Kron-Hewit, which is the number one medical supply firm internationally. As the story goes, Kron was a genius at inventing medical products, and Hewit was a marketing genius. So, they joined forces some 60 years ago and slowly built the company into its current leadership position. Dave was quickly "fast tracked" at Kron, moving up rapidly in marketing, then three years in general operations in Singapore, four more years in charge of setting up operations in Eastern Europe, and then back in the States for four years as the head of their hospital supply division.

However, at that point it was pretty clear, at least in Dave's mind, that his upward ride at Kron had probably ended. He loved the company, but there didn't seem to be any room to move up. The people ahead of him in the leadership structure were about his age and not going to move on for a few years. Plus, there was a slew of "fast trackers" in the pipeline eagerly waiting for their shot at the top positions. So, when MMS contacted him about running their business, he didn't think twice. The company was young, was growing rapidly, he knew the medical supply business, and was ready to lead.

He had flown to Denver to see Carrie Bozak, the CEO of Hathorn Medical Systems, a five hospital system in the Southwest U.S. with corporate headquarters in Denver. Carrie had asked him to meet with her this morning to discuss what she described as a "matter of utmost importance that could not be discussed on the phone." Hathorn was one of MMS's loyal customers, probably to the tune of $3 to $4 million in annual sales. So Carrie could not be ignored, and he flew to Denver early that morning. This was the start of the Memorial Day weekend, and he had hoped for a quick meeting with Carrie, an early flight out of Denver, and maybe even to make it back home to take his wife out to dinner and a movie.

The "matter of utmost importance" that Carrie wanted to talk about was the outcome of an internal review of the Hathorn purchasing unit. It appeared, and she repeatedly emphasized the word "appears," that some questionable (again, emphasizing "questionable") practices occurred in the purchases Hathorn made from MMS and other suppliers. While she was very cautious not to accuse anyone directly, the bottom line was that it appeared that one or more of her purchasing people had been receiving kickbacks from suppliers. And one of the chief suspects was Red Morgan, who was the MMS district sales manager for the Southwest area.

While Dave suspected that Red probably was guilty as accused, that was something he could not say to Carrie. Instead, he went through a song and dance about how shocked he was to even think that MMS might be involved in anything unethical. He told her about the MMS ethics code which was "the toughest in the industry," and to which every MMS employee is totally committed.

He went on to assure her that he would launch an immediate investigation. "We simply won't tolerate anything unethical in our company," he said. The meeting ended with Dave telling Carrie how important the Hathorn business was to MMS. Carrie seemed impressed with his presentation, and Dave left the meeting thinking that he may have dodged the bullet on this one.

In the cab ride to the airport, Dave pondered how he was going to broach this issue with Red. He really dreaded talking to Red, particularly about an issue like this. Morgan was difficult at best. In the company he was known as "Redbeard the Pirate" for the short stubble of a reddish beard that he wore, as well as for his questionable sales techniques. As far as Red was concerned, the only thing that mattered was closing the sale, and how you accomplished that was not important. Red had been with the company since its beginning, had built up some great customer contacts, and consequently saw himself as someone who couldn't be touched in the sales unit. He didn't get along with his boss, the vice president of sales and marketing. In fact, he rarely spoke to her. When Red wanted something he usually contacted Dave rather than his boss, although the discussion usually ended at an impasse with Red saying that people like Dave "really didn't understand the sales process" and therefore "should keep their nose out of things they don't understand."

But since Red made his sales numbers every quarter—in fact, had been one of the better sales producers—he was tolerated, however reluctantly. The sales people are paid a base salary plus a commission on what they sell, and they are eligible for an end-of-the-year bonus. All of this is based on making a quarterly sales quota. Red rarely missed his quota.

But right now Dave was stuck in Denver. It looked like at least a two-hour delay at this point, probably more. First priority is to call my wife, Dave thought, and cancel the evening out. She would understand, sort of. However, Dave felt that he had spent much of the last year canceling their nights out, and apologizing for it.

This also may be a good time to call Anita McCall, vice president for sales and marketing, and brief her on the conversation with Carrie. Maybe ask for her suggestions on how to handle it. But I am probably the one to talk to Red about the problem, Dave thought. Red and Anita just don't get along and any conversation between them will be a disaster. At least Red will talk to me, even though he thinks my knowledge of the sales function is extremely limited and naïve.

He also thought of calling Red. Maybe if I can get a hold of Anita, I can try Red after that and see if I can get this mess off of the table today, he thought. But then he decided to wait until Tuesday. While he rationalized that both would probably not be in their offices given the Memorial Day weekend, the reality was that he was just too tired and too frustrated to deal with the whole incident.

As he slumped in one of those uncomfortable molded plastic seats in the crowded terminal, he started to think about the job and about MMS. This is not fun, he thought, so why do I do this? It is just one hassle after another—product recalls, audit problems, a key customer canceling, alleged kick backs, and who knows what. This job is one big problem after another.

On the other hand, working at Kron had been fun. It seemed something new and interesting was always happening—always new challenges, and new hurdles. And there was great support. There was always someone you could turn to, someone with both experience and wisdom. Like Charlie Schaefer, who ended up as the number two person at Kron, and who had been his mentor there. He first met Charlie in Hong Kong, where Charlie headed up the Far East operations. Charlie was a guy you could talk with. He always had time for you, and you always knew he was 100% on your side. When he was at Kron, Dave would email or call Charlie probably once a week or so, sometimes just to say hi, other times for advice.

Maybe that is the difference now. There are no Charlie Schaefers at MMS. There isn't anyone at MMS I can talk with in an open and honest way.

Actually, there isn't anyone here I can really trust. Kron had a family culture, a culture that was big on mutual support. MMS doesn't have support culture. It probably doesn't have a culture at all.

The more he reflected, the more he started thinking that maybe he had made a mistake in coming to MMS. It looked so good in the beginning, but the dream now looked more like a nightmare. Maybe it would have been better to stay at Kron. He may not have become the CEO, but at least he would have been happy with his work.

He wondered if there might be a place for him back at Kron. After all, he was one of their shining stars at one time, and he left on good terms, so why not? The more he thought about this idea, the more it made sense to him.

As he thought of who he might talk to about this, about the only name that popped into his mind was Charlie Schaefer. Charlie was retired now, although was doing some part-time consulting. He lived with his wife on about three acres of land about 30 minutes from Dave's house. Charlie was still well connected at Kron and was called back on occasion to provide the voice of experience. Charlie was someone he could trust to give him a straight answer. If it was a stupid idea, Charlie would tell him that it was stupid. So Dave got his cell phone out and punched in Charlie's number.

"Dave, where the heck have you been?" Charlie said. "It has probably been six months since I heard from you. How's the job going?"

"Well, that's why I called," said Dave. "I am not too happy here and was looking for some advice. By the way, I am in the Denver airport and in the middle of a rain delay, so I have some time to talk. How about you?"

"Actually, I am on my way out the door," Charlie said, "but what are you doing Monday, Memorial Day? Why don't you and Nancy come out to see us on the farm—we are only about 30 minutes from your home. We are not doing anything on Monday, and I promise to cook up some of my famous barbeque ribs for you."

"I was thinking of going in the office Monday, just to catch up on some things," Dave responded.

"Forget the office." Charlie retorted. "You said you weren't happy, so how is going to the office going to improve your happiness? It will probably just make it worse. Sounds like you need to relax. So, why don't you take it easy on Monday and come out and see us about 1:00 p.m.?"

"You sold me! Nancy and I will be there," said Dave, "and I am really looking forward to seeing you." That ended the conversation, and as Dave put the cell phone in his pocket, he felt a strange sense of relief come over him. "Everything is going to be all right," he said to himself. "Charlie will know what to do!"

2

Memorial Day at Charlie Schaefer's Farm

Charlie's farm is not what most people would refer to as a farm. It consists of a ranch style house with a connecting three car garage, which sits on about three acres of land. There is large patio at the rear of the house with a huge barbeque cooker and a couple of tables with umbrellas and chairs. A field of short grass with a patch of trees toward the back is all there is to the rest of the "farm." Babe is the only animal Charlie keeps—an old dog who spends most of her time sunning on the patio.

Charlie loves to cook, and on Monday afternoon he was at his best— ribs, chicken breasts, and corn. His wife made her special salad with fruit and nuts in it, and the desert was her homemade peach cobbler.

As they ate, the table conversation was mainly about old Kron friends, and after Charlie had cleared the plates he announced, "Hey ladies, Dave and I have something important to talk about so we are going to take little walk around the property," and signaled Dave to follow him.

They probably hadn't taken three steps off of the patio when Charlie said in his usual direct manner, "So, what's the problem my friend? I think

Becoming a Values-Based Leader, pages 7–11
Copyright © 2012 by Information Age Publishing

the last time I talked with you, you were feeling pretty good about the job. What's happened in the last six months to change that?

"Well," Dave said, "let me give you a list of my problems." As they walked Dave told Charlie about the problems with Red, about the latest product recall, about the outside auditors, plus a handful of other issues that would be on Dave's desk tomorrow morning.

"When I was hired for this CEO job I was told that they were looking for a chief problem-solver, that's what CEOs do. They solve all of the big problems that can't get solved anywhere else in the organization. Well, I have tried to do that, but, quite frankly, the problems pile keeps growing bigger and bigger, and the issues seem to be getting more and more serious."

"Last week was the worst I have had since I have been at MMS," Dave continued, "and at this point I have had enough!"

Charlie was silent for a moment and seemed to be deep in thought. Then he said, "So how can I help? What can I do to help you with this? What do you want from me?"

"The reason I called you Friday is that I was thinking of resigning from MMS, and then seeing if I could go back to Kron. I spent most of my career at Kron and really am comfortable with the place. My leaving Kron, I am thinking now, was big a mistake."

"Wow!" exclaimed Charlie, "You really have been doing some heavy thinking!"

Charlie fell silent again, then he slowly said, "How long have we known each other?"

"It must be at least fifteen years, ever since you were heading the Far East operations in Hong Kong. You became my mentor and friend," Dave replied.

"And mentors and friend should be totally honest, shouldn't they?" Charlie asked.

"I hope so," Dave responded, "that is the only way they can be helpful."

"Well, then," Charlie said, "let me give you an honest opinion.

"First, let's talk about you returning to Kron. I would advise against it. Maybe they would rehire you, maybe they would not, I don't know. But if they did, it wouldn't be the same. You no longer would be one of the fast trackers who are in line for the choice positions. You were replaced a long time ago in the leadership pipeline. They have a long list of talented men and women that they are paying special attention to now.

"And let me be very blunt, if they thought that reason you are coming back is because the MMS leadership position didn't work out, they would conclude that you had your shot at top leadership, but didn't make it. So, why should they give you a choice position, or even groom you for one? You had your shot at the major leagues and blew it. So, they aren't about to groom you for a second shot."

"Ouch," said Dave. "That hurts, but if you are correct, that's not going to be a way to go! But what are my options? Stick with MMS and keep suffering?"

"No, I think the best option is not to stay with MMS and keep suffering. Your best option is to stay with MMS and get your act together and have some fun," Charlie responded.

"What do you mean?" asked Dave.

Charlie was very serious, "You have been telling me about all of the problems you are having at MMS. About the problem with Red Morgan, and the problem with manufacturing, and the one with your accounting people and so on. Am I correct? "

"Right," said Dave.

"Well, let me be blunt. I don't think they are the problem," Charlie said rather quietly. "I think the problem is you. You are the problem."

"What are you talking about?" asked Dave, "I don't understand!"

"The problem is that you are not leading," Charlie responded. "Whoever the idiot was that said you should be the chief problem solver in the organization should be shot. They hired you to lead, not to solve everyone's problems.

"No wonder you are tired and frustrated. I would be too. It sounds like your office is a dumping ground for problems. You spend your time running around putting out fires. How could you not be worn out?" he continued.

"Look at the issue with Red Morgan. You are trying to make everybody happy—you are trying to make Red happy, and make Anita happy, and make the person from the hospital happy. In the first place, you can't make everyone happy—it's an impossible task. But more important, that is not your job at MMS. Morgan is Anita's issue, not yours. You shouldn't have touched the Morgan problem! In your eagerness to be helpful, you undercut Anita's authority."

Dave was silent. Charlie's words cut deep. He didn't really know what to say. Was Charlie correct?

"Hear me out," Charlie continued. "You need to forget the chief problem solver nonsense, and forget trying to make everybody happy, and start leading.

"You can do it. Kron spent 20 years and a heck of a lot of money grooming you to lead. You might not be at Kron, but now is the time to use those skills and knowledge. It is time to apply your leadership skills and training!"

They were back at the patio now, and Charlie signaled Dave to sit with him in one of the lounge chairs. The women had gone into the house as the weather had turned a little chilly.

They sat in silence for a while, and then Dave said, "I guess I really don't know where to go from here. You are probably right, or at least you make sense, although I will have to think more about it. But I am not sure of the next step. I am meeting with Anita first thing tomorrow morning, what do you suggest I do? Should I fire Red?"

"I am not going to suggest anything to you," Charlie responded. "You have to decide what to do. It is your decision. Although I would state that firing Red is not going to ease your problem. Your problem is leadership, not Red.

"However, I would suggest the name of someone who you might talk to. Do you remember Rena Lopez, who did some of our leadership coaching work at Kron?"

Dave said he vaguely remembered the name. He thought he had taken a workshop from her a few years back, although couldn't remember what the workshop was about. But he knew she had a great reputation as a leadership coach.

"Well, she is still in the area, and still helps us out at Kron," said Charlie. "I have her number inside. I think you need some help in sorting this out, and in my mind she's one of the best coaches in the business! She has worked with the top people at Kron, I think very effectively."

Just then Nancy appeared and reminded Dave that it was starting to get late and it was time to head home. They said their goodbyes and thanked Charlie and his wife for their hospitality. On the way out Charlie gave Dave the phone number for Rena.

"I hope that I wasn't too blunt," Charlie said to Dave quietly as he was leaving, "but this was a discussion between two old friends."

"No, I really appreciate your frankness." said Dave, "However, it is going to take me some time to sort out what you said. And believe me, I cherish our friendship."

As they drove home, Dave was unusually silent.

"You are very quiet," Nancy commented, "What happened between you and Charlie? Is something wrong?"

"No, everything is okay. We just talked about some business issues and I guess I still am thinking about them," Dave answered.

He hadn't told Nancy about his problems at MMS, or even about his recent thoughts about returning to Kron. He suspected that she knew things weren't going well because she had commented a couple of times recently that he seemed very stressed.

He kept thinking back to Charlie's statement that Red wasn't the problem, but that he, Dave, was the problem. Ouch, that was hard to accept. Nobody wants to hear that he is the problem

On the other hand, he respected Charlie's opinion. Charlie was a good friend and had been a very successful leader. He, Dave, would have to sort that out. Maybe talking with Rena was not such a bad idea. Actually, she seemed to be his best option—maybe his only option at this point.

3

The First Meeting with Rena
What Is This Values Thing All About?

Whoever designed these suburban office parks must have loved fun-house mazes as a kid, murmured Dave as he seemingly drove in circles looking for Rena's office building.

He had called her early Tuesday morning and told her that he had been thinking of resigning from MMS and maybe trying to hook up with Kron again, and also of his conversation with Charlie.

She said she thought she remembered him from her work at Kron, and further indicated that she thought they ought to get together fairly quickly given that he was thinking of resigning from MMS. She had an opening on Thursday afternoon, and Dave rearranged his schedule to meet at that time.

So, if he could ever find his way through the maze of winding streets and parking lots, he would be able to meet with her.

As he thought about what they might discuss, he acknowledged to himself that this week was going much better than the last one. One reason was that the product recall was not as serious as they had anticipated. Only a short product run of about 300 units was involved, which could easily be replaced. And it was caught before any of it got to a patient. However, Dave thought that the recall was a warning sign that all was not right at that manufacturing plant. They seemed to reject a lot of product at final inspection, and occasionally some of it slipped through and got sent to the customer.

He had also met with Anita on Tuesday morning and briefed her about the conversation he had with Carrie Bozak. Anita seemed to take it in stride. She told him that she had heard rumors that Red had been pretty generous with his gift giving over the last year. Since she and Red don't talk much she said she didn't know the details, although did know that he had been handing out a lot of free tickets to the pro basketball games in Denver and Los Angles. She didn't know what else he might have handed out, given that Red was very secretive about how he handled his sales.

Anita said that she would get in touch with Carrie Bozak to find out what they had found out on their end, and would also try to talk to Red to get his version of the story. However, since Red usually didn't return her messages she was not too optimistic that she would get Red's version of the problem.

Dave had mixed feelings about the meeting with Anita. On one hand she seemed to be understanding of the situation and would follow-up with Carrie and Red. On the other hand, nothing had changed—they still had no solution to the "Red problem."

He finally found Rena's office building with about five minutes to spare.

Rena greeted him warmly and they talked briefly about the old days at Kron. After that short discussion, Rena said she first wanted to catch up on his career and wanted to know where he had been and what he had been doing. So Dave briefed her about his career moves at Kron and then moving to the CEO position at MMS.

"Wow," she exclaimed, "you have really been busy since I saw you last. And it sounds like things have been going great for you. You are sort of a poster boy for how to make good career moves. So, what's the problem?"

"Well, as I mentioned to you on the phone, things haven't quite worked out the way I anticipated that they would at MMS," Dave responded.

"So, tell me about it," Rena said.

Given that lead, Dave spent the next 45 minutes telling Rena about the problems at MMS. He elaborated in some detail about the problems in manufacturing, the loss of a key customer, and the continuing problems with Red.

"Probably the best way to summarize this experience," he said, "is that I feel like my life is spent putting out fires that never seem to go out completely. You know those trick candles that sometimes are put on birthday cakes—the ones that when the person blows them out, they go out for a second or two, and then flare up again. Trying to blow them out is a lesson in futility—they never will go out."

"That's me!" he continued. "The same problems keep flaring up. It's no fun. It is nothing but frustration. Red is a good example—once you put out a fire he started, he starts another one the next week."

Rena seemed to understand, or at least she nodded in understanding. When he finished, she said, "You told me that you were really excited when you first took over as CEO of MMS. Do you think being the CEO of MMS could be an exciting job given the right conditions?"

Dave thought a couple of seconds, and then said, "Well, maybe. I don't really know. I mean the company has great potential. No question, the potential is there. But, I am really not. . . ."

Before Dave could finish the sentence, Rena said, "That's great! Then we have something to work on, don't we? Our target is to return the excitement of the job. It sounds like both the job and the company have a great deal of potential!"

Before Dave could answer, she continued, "I would like to explain a bit about how I work, so you know what to expect from me. I think some leaders are pretty shallow and make it up as they go along. They are often pretty glib and say all the right things. But they don't have any strong beliefs or values. Rather, they are like chameleons and change their beliefs and values to fit the situation. I don't think these people last long in a leadership position. People catch on pretty quickly that there is nothing there but a lot of show.

"In contrast, all effective leaders have a great deal of character and have strongly held beliefs and values. Just look at the great leaders of history, like Martin Luther King or Lincoln or Churchill, or whoever. Or look at the great leaders in business, or the great athletic coaches. They knew who they were and what they believed in, and their values guided their behavior and decisions—they were, in my mind, values-based leaders in that they led with their values.

"So, my approach as a coach is to help people discover, or actually to help them rediscover, their values and character. It takes a little time. I am not into the quick fix, because quick fixes don't work. We have to spend a little time rediscovering oneself and one's values."

"And finally," she continued, "I am completely confident that in a couple of months you will change your attitude about the job and the company. In fact, I am pretty confident that you will begin to see the CEO position and the company as an exciting opportunity. But first, we need to connect you with your values.

"Questions?" she asked.

Dave just shook his head. Actually he was speechless. He was trying to digest what Rena had just said and wasn't really sure he understood the approach. On one hand, it did make sense, but on the other hand it did not.

"Good, let's end with that. I am sure you will have more questions later," she said. "And I have a homework assignment for you for next time—nothing very heavy. I would like you to tell me who the four or five people were that most significantly impacted your life, and what you learned from them that was so important. Specifically, what you learned from them that you would like to emulate. The people you list can be people from your childhood, or school, or work, or even historical figures."

The assignment momentarily stunned Dave. "Wait," he said, "aren't we going to talk about some of my problems? For example, aren't we going to talk about Red?"

"Red who?" Rena said with a broad smile on her face, "I never heard of a Red. This isn't about Red. As I said, this is all about Dave, and that's you. So, why should we talk about Red? Let's meet again next week, and don't forget your assignment," she added.

And with that reply, they said their goodbyes.

As Dave left the building and headed toward his car, he puzzled over the meeting with Rena, and especially about the assignment he was given. He had fully expected that his meeting with Rena would focus on how he should deal with some of his problems. Isn't that what coaches are supposed to do? However, Rena didn't seem to be very interested in his problems. And she never even brought up the subject of his quitting and going back to Kron—that was odd. Finally, he thought about the assignment she gave him—what the heck was that all about?

On the other hand, he was intrigued by Rena's question about whether the job could be exciting again given the right circumstances. He hadn't thought about that. Yes, it probably could. And he felt good about the fact that that she seemed optimistic when she said that this gives us a target—to make the job exciting again. Maybe this will work out okay!

HOMEWORK ASSIGNMENT

Who were (are) the Important People in your Life

Who were (are) the four or five people who most significantly impacted your life? Briefly describe each. Why were they important in your life? What did you learn from them that you would like to emulate?

4

Who Are the Important People in Your Life?

The next week seemed to have passed quickly, Dave thought. No new crises. Actually, it was a quiet week at work. The fact that a few people in the office had been off on vacation probably helped a bit.

As Dave headed for his appointment with Rena, he thought to himself that he had been feeling much better this week. But he couldn't figure out just why. Maybe it was because the quiet week at the office. Or, he wondered, could it be that some of the things that Rena talked about were actually helping him? However, he couldn't point to specifically what she said or did that would have accounted for the change in his outlook on life.

He liked the assignment she gave him, which was to list the four or five people who had been a major impact on his life and what Dave had learned from them. Actually, the assignment was an "upper," in that it made him think back to better times and some of the pleasant experiences of his life. He couldn't wait to tell Rena about some of the people on his list.

Becoming a Values-Based Leader, pages 19–27
Copyright © 2012 by Information Age Publishing
19

This time he found office building without much problem and found Rena waiting for him.

"Did you do your homework assignment?" she asked in a cheery voice as he walked into her office.

"Yes, teacher," he jokingly replied. "So, can I go to my desk now?"

"Definitely," she responded, laughing. "I might even give you a gold star or a smiley face if I like your paper."

After they talked briefly about a mutual acquaintance—one of the key managers at Kron who had just taken an early retirement to open a bed and breakfast—she asked him, "So, tell me about people who had an impact on your life and what you learned from them."

"Well, number one was my father," Dave replied. "I think I really learned a lot from him..." and he went on to elaborate. He talked about his father serving in the infantry in Vietnam, and then coming back to the suburb that had been his hometown to work for an uncle who had a small grocery store. A couple years after his dad joined the business, the uncle decided to retire and move south, and his dad took over.

"I think dad bought the business for $500," Dave said. "The stock on the shelves was probably worth twice that or more. So, Dad went into the grocery business, and by default so did my sisters and I—we worked there on Saturdays and during vacations.

"Some of dad's ideas, maybe you could call them values, really stuck with me.

"He believed it was important was to work hard, to give the customer what they wanted, and always do the right thing. He probably told me that ten times a week. That was his business philosophy, and that's how he ran the business.

"He worked 10 to 12 hours a day, six days a week. He really believed if you worked hard, things would work out. He said that nobody was going to give you anything for free—you are going to have to work for it. So, for him, hard work was the key to success, and he was very successful in the business.

"Customer service was his top priority. He would tell the staff to always remember that the customer pays our salary, never forget that! Another of his favorite sayings was—serve one customer at a time. This meant that we were to treat each customer as a unique individual and to serve each of their unique needs as best we could.

"When he talked about doing the right thing he meant treating everybody fairly and with respect. And he had absolutely no tolerance for any cheating or anything like that. I remember the time he found out that one of the delivery guys was stealing groceries from the deliveries. The guy was fired on the spot.

"But probably above all was his love for family. I had two sisters and, of course, a mom. Dad was devoted to us. He never missed a birthday, or family event, and used to sneak away from the store in the afternoons to see the kids perform at school. He was always home with us in the evening, and Sunday was church day, and sometimes we had gatherings of the extended family on Sunday. His life was family first, and then the store."

"I am really impressed," Rena said. "He really had an influence on you. But, which of those lessons that you learned from your father do you want to emulate or to become part of your legacy?"

"Well, I can tell you one that I guess I inherited from him, and that is hard work." Dave responded. "I always have put in 10 to 12 hour work days. I don't know if that is good or bad, but it is my father in me.

"Another lesson I learned from him is the importance of family. And another one is treating everyone fairly. I think I do, but haven't really thought about it. I hope I do.

"Can I share one more thing about him?" Dave asked.

"Go ahead, I'm enjoying this," Rena said. "I am really impressed with your Dad."

"One thing I really admired about him was after he was in business about 25 years, the town had grown such that it attracted some of the big grocery chains. They put up a Jewel in the center of town and a Super Wal-Mart just at the edge of town. That took its toll on the business and he eventually had to close the grocery store and sell the property.

"But what was amazing was that he wasn't bitter at all. He said that he thanked God for 25 good years of business. And he said that progress just moves on and that's that. It's no use blaming somebody, or crying about it. You have to move on too. So, he did move on and went on to a second career as the office manager for a friend's construction business, and he loved that job."

"That's a great way to look at things. Actually, it's a very positive and constructive way to deal with adversity," Rena said, and added, "If you can't do anything about it, then move on. I wish more people would take that approach. But let's go on. Who is next on your list?"

"My mom is next on my list." Dave continued, "She was probably the unsung hero in my life. I think we take moms for granted because they are always there. My mom was always there when we needed her. She kept the house, and raised the kids, and helped out at the store when she was needed. Interestingly enough, she was the finance person in the family and made sure the household and the store were always in the black.

"But one important lesson my mother taught me was to be a learner. She thought education was important—not only the type you learn in school, but more importantly, the lessons you learn in life. She was always asking the question, what did you learn, and how can you use that learning? She taught me that there is a valuable lesson to be learned in most every experience.

"I remember one time failing a math test. I think I was in 8th grade. I thought she would yell at me but she didn't. She just asked me what I learned from that experience. Actually, I hadn't studied for the test because some friends and I were trying to form a rock band and were busy trying to memorize some song for the school talent contest. I learned that one has to prioritize things in life, and studying for a math test should been my number one priority, and once that was finished I could spend time with the rock band."

"Sounds like she taught you a very valuable lesson," Rena said, "But, tell me, how good was your rock band?"

"Terrible!" Dave replied quickly, "We had cool costumes, but didn't know how to play any instruments. So that lasted all of three months."

"I take it that being a life-long learner is the lesson that you would like to take from your mom," Rena said.

"Yep," Dave agreed, "always keep learning, and also make sure you do the important things first."

"Jenny Ingberg, my first boss at Kron, is next on my list," Dave continued. "She really had an impact at a critical period in my life. Right after college I spent almost two years at a company that is now defunct, and it really soured me on the world of business. The people running the company were really sleazy—they cheated everyone—customers, employees, suppliers, and the government. It was a terrible experience for me and I bailed out quickly.

"So, I began to think that the world of business seemed corrupt and was not for me, and I was actually toying with going back to school to study law. The problem was that I didn't have any money, and had some college loans to pay off, so I needed a job quickly. A buddy told me that Kron was a great place to work and was hiring. So, I signed up.

"Jenny would preach to the new recruits about the important role of business in society, as well as the special mission of Kron. She would talk to us about the Kron vision and values.

"Wow! She was inspirational! She not only restored my faith in business, but really made me want to be a part of the future of Kron. I really thought that the company had a special mission, and I wanted to be part of it. Kron had a purpose and direction, and it gave me a purpose and direction, and as a new recruit I was convinced that neither of us could be stopped."

"Do you still believe that?" Rena interrupted. "Do you think you believe the same about your current company, and yourself, now? That you and the company have a special purpose and a direction?"

"That's an interesting question," Dave said rather slowly, "I don't know. I don't think I have ever thought about it that much. I guess I really don't know."

"Sounds like something we might talk about sometime," Rena said. "But not now. Tell me, what part of the Jenny experience do you want to make part of your life?"

"The part that believes that businesses have a special purpose and a mission. The inspirational and motivational piece. I wish I could convey that message to all of my team and all of my company. That would be awesome!"

"Again, something we might talk about later," Rena responded. "But who is next on your list?"

"Well, you know the next person, that's Charlie Schaefer," Dave continued. "What can I say about him? He had a tremendous impact on my life. He was my boss for over six years, and remained a friend and mentor.

"What did I learn from him? Well, a ton of stuff. He was open, and honest, and blunt, and demanded the best out of everyone, and was a stickler for doing things right. But I think what I admire most about him was that he was a fantastic people developer. Just about everybody who worked for Charlie really advanced in his or her career.

"To use today's buzz word, Charlie empowered people. He didn't tell you what to do; rather, he helped you in deciding what needed to be done, as well as figuring out the best way to do it. You were on your own, almost. Working with Charlie was a fantastic learning experience. You learned to deal with issues, to think things out, to take responsibility, and to learn from your mistakes. That's where I really learned to stand on my own two feet and to take charge. I wish all of my employees at MMS could have had the same experience that I did with Charlie. If Charlie had trained them, I doubt that we would have the problems we are having now.

"What did I learn from Charlie that I would like to emulate?" Dave continued. "People development! He was the best, and is still at it as evidenced by his recommending that I come to you. I wish I could be at least half as good as Charlie was at people development."

"Well, that's my A list." said Dave with a feeling of satisfaction. "What do you think?"

"I am really impressed," Rena answered. "Those are some great stories. You have had some great teachers, and your teachers had some great values. But I would also add that it is clear that you are a great learner. Someone once said that leadership can't be taught, but it can be learned. I think you learned your lessons well. Congratulations!"

"Well, thank you. It was a great assignment. I really enjoyed it, and it connected me back to some good times and good people. So, what do we do next?" Dave asked.

"Well, I want to give you another homework assignment," Rena said.

"Oh, no! Not another assignment!" Dave responded, pretending to be offended.

"Oh, yes," said Rena, "and this one is a bit tougher.

"The purpose of the assignment you just completed was to get you thinking about values, particularly the values and lessons of people who were important to you. Now I want to take this a bit further. What I want you to do now is to list your life values. What five of six values are the most important to you in life? I am not talking about leadership values or work values. I mean life values.

"I also would like you to tell me what you want to accomplish in life. What's important to you? What is your purpose in life?"

"Wow!" said Dave. "That is tough. I don't think I ever thought about that, although I once went to a workshop where we were asked to write our obituaries and we were to include what we had hoped to accomplish in life."

"This is not quite the same," Rena replied, "obits are looking at the past. I want you to look at the future. But first, let's talk about values. When I ask you to talk about your values, what does that mean to you? What's a value?"

"Boy, you ask tough questions" Dave replied. "Well, let me see if I can answer that. I know a value is something good and something important. And it is not very specific. For example, if I say I have strong family values, or I value my family, that is very general. It says that my family is very important to me, and in the grand scheme of things I would put my family ahead of a lot of things. So, I guess values are also priorities, but very general priorities. They are guides to our behavior."

"How about this?" Dave continued. "Values are important ideas or principles that provide the criteria for our choices and priorities in life and at work. I think I like that definition."

DAVE'S DEFINITION OF VALUES

Values are important ideas or principles that provide the criteria for our choices and priorities in life and work.

"Nice! I like your idea about values being priorities," Rena responded. "Values help us make choices; they tell us what is important in a given situation. But aren't there hundreds of values out there? For example, look at some of the things you talked about today—they seem to be values—hard work, doing the right thing, serving the customers, empowerment, family, and the list could go on and on. If they are all priorities, how do I decide among the priorities?"

"Oh, I see where you are going," said Dave. "I think I would answer that by saying that there may be values for different areas that apply mostly to that area. For example, we could talk about one's political values in a broad sense such as conservative or liberal, or you could talk about your work values like I did with my father. Different situations may arouse a different set of values."

"But I asked you to list your life values, the values that are most important in your life," Rena continued. "Does that make sense in terms of what you just said? Are there such things as life values?"

"Definitely, or at least I think so," Dave responded. "I think that there are values that are central to a person's life, or at least I think that many people have set of core values that are really important in their life. Maybe not everyone has as set of life values, but I think the effective people do. I am thinking of people like Martin Luther King. I hadn't really thought of it until you just brought it up, but I am now thinking that it is those people who have a clear set of life values or core values who make the biggest impact in this world.

"It is not just the Martin Luther Kings of the world, but the more I think of it I believe that even the everyday people who make a contribution to their community or to their work have a set of strong core values. I can think of people like Charlie, and Jenny, and my Dad, or my kids' teachers. They seem to know what's important in their lives and have an overall goal or a purpose. They know who they are and know what they want to accomplish in life. They are driven by purpose and values.

"Hey," Dave continued, "you are making a believer out of me. I came in here today a little suspicious as to what this was all about, and it looks like I will be leaving as a true believer. You sold me!"

"Actually, my job here is not to sell you on anything, but rather it is to get you thinking about life and careers," Rena responded. "It was to make sense to you. I take it that you are comfortable with your assignment?"

"I am, thanks to our brief discussion," Dave said. "I will work on my purpose in life, and come up with a list of my life values. How many values should I list?"

"You will know," said Rena. "Most people don't go beyond five or six. Remember, we are only looking for the really important core values that help you establish the priorities in your life."

"Got it!" Dave replied. "But I still want to know when we are going to talk about Red," he added jokingly.

"Red who?" Rena answered with a laugh. "I never heard of a Red. See you next week. And don't forget the assignment."

As they parted company, Dave felt that he was starting to understand what this was all about. It wasn't about Red Morgan at all, or anyone else. It was about Dave. It was about who Dave was and what he believed. Great session, he thought as he walked toward his car. And this next assignment should really be interesting.

HOMEWORK ASSIGNMENT

What is Your Purpose in Life?

What is your life purpose? What would you like to accomplish in your life? Why would it be important (to you) to accomplish that?

HOMEWORK ASSIGNMENT

What are Your Life Values?

What are your five or six most important life values? These are the values that you would use to guide your life.

How would you "walk the talk" on each of these values? That is, if you were living these values to the fullest, what would we see you doing?

5

What Are Your Life Values?

The next week went by very quickly for Dave. He spent much of the week prepping for a presentation for an analysts' meeting in New York, but also found time to take a day off to go shopping with his wife for some new kitchen appliances.

He noted that he was feeling pretty good as he drove to his meeting with Rena. Actually, this was the best he had felt in a long time. He was looking forward to today's meeting with Rena as he had a lot to report. He had spent a lot more time thinking about values than he had anticipated.

After exchanging greetings with Rena, he told her that had a very interesting experience on Saturday night that he wanted to share with her.

"Two couples from the neighborhood came over on Saturday night for a relaxing evening of some pizza and talk. Early in the evening someone asked me if I had done anything interesting lately and I mentioned that I was working with a coach and she gave me a very interesting assignment, which was to define my values.

Becoming a Values-Based Leader, pages 29–39
Copyright © 2012 by Information Age Publishing
29

"They picked up on that right away and someone said why don't we all try that and have each person list their top five or six values? Then they added another twist and said why don't we guess what everybody else put down as their top values? Then we can compare what we had actually put down with what others thought we put down.

"It turned out to be a lot of fun. Values such as family, personal achievement and financial success were on many of the lists. However, I did learn an important lesson and that is not to assume that everyone else shares your values. I think I assumed that everyone would have approximately the same values, particularly since we live in the same community. But that was not the case.

"I completely blew it in predicting the values of one of my neighbors. He is in advertising and she is an elementary school teacher. The top value for both of them was creativity and I think social justice was next. Values like achievement and financial success were not even on their list."

"That is a great lesson to remember," replied Rena. "We sort of assume that most people have the same values as ours, but that is not necessarily true. If we are going to really understand others we have to get beyond our inherent assumptions that they are like us in values, and begin to appreciate their ways of looking at the world."

"And there seemed to be some interesting differences between the men and women," Dave continued. "For example, we got into some interesting discussions over what values would take priority over what other values. Would family always take priority over personal achievement or visa versa? The women seemed to think personal achievement was a dominant value for most men and that men would sacrifice family for achievement. But they thought that for most women, if push came to shove, women would always put family first over everything else. As you might expect, that led to a rather heated debate between the men and the women. It turned out to be a fun evening that also had a serious side, because it forced us to think about our values and or our values choices.

"We ended up by joking that we thought we had invented a new parlor game, or maybe a TV game show, called 'What's Your Values' and we were going to copyright it and make a fortune. That idea in itself may say something, perhaps not too flattering, about our values."

"Sounds like you really got into it," Rena responded.

"We really did. I won't go into all that they said about me, although I will tell you that I have been home for dinner every night this week, which is definitely a change from my usual behavior," Dave said.

"Well, enough of that," Dave continued. "Would you like to hear about what I want to accomplish in life?"

"Definitely," said Rena.

"I really thought a lot about this and I went through several lists that included a great family, and a nice house, and a lot of money, and a bunch of other things.

"But, in the end it came down to one central theme and that is that I want to make a positive impact or to have a positive influence. I want to be a contributor. I realize that this is not earth shaking, like finding a cure for cancer, but I think it is honest in that it is me.

"I want to make a positive impact on my family—to be a good husband and father. And to be a positive impact in my community—to contribute to the community, and the schools, and my kids' youth athletic teams—to make them more healthy and successful.

"The same with my work life. I want to have a positive impact at work—to help make MMS the premier company in our industry. And to positively impact our employees and also the customers we serve.

"As I mentioned before, I don't think that my purpose statement is very earth shaking or exciting. But it is what I really want to do. It is what I am all about," Dave concluded.

DAVE'S PURPOSE IN LIFE

To make a positive contribution or to have a positive influence on the people I associate with, and the organizations I am part of. They will be much better for my being part of their lives.

"Hey, don't apologize," said Rena. "You really have put some time and thought into this assignment. Congratulations! I think it is a great purpose! My next question is, why or how does that purpose energize you? Why is it motivating?"

"Good question," Dave responded. "I am not sure I have a good answer except to say that I have always wanted to be a contributor. I always wanted to make a positive contribution whether it was in the family store, or in the family, or at work. It makes me feel good to know that I am making a contribution and improving lives or improving organizations. Does that make sense?"

"It makes perfect sense," Rena replied. "Very often, people can't explain why a purpose is energizing or motivating, but they know that it is.

It just feels good! But let's move on to your top life values. I am anxious to hear what you put down."

"Okay," Dave answered, "but let me preface this by saying that I tried to decide which were my five top life values. Now that was really tough. Actually, there seem to be several that are at the top, and I can't really list them in any order."

Rena responded, "That's typical; all values are all good—that's why we call them values. And most people find it difficult to narrow the list to four or five. So, what's on your short list?"

"Well, family is one of the top values," Dave continued. "It's all about being close to my wife and my children, and also our extended family. My dad is dead but my mother is still going strong, and my sister and her husband have several children.

"There is no question that I owe my success to my family. I think that is true for every successful person. My family not only gave me all of the basics, but more importantly, there was always a lot of love and support. You could always count on them. I really think that family is the key to a better future, both for individuals and for communities. If a kid has a strong family, he or she is bound to be a success. If a community is made up of strong families, it is bound to be a great community.

"And I am not talking only about the traditional Mom and Dad families. There are a lot of very strong single parent families around."

"Another of my top values is education." Dave continued.

"Whoa! Let's hold up on that one," said Rena. "I want to know how one walks the walk on the family value, particularly how Dave walks the walk. What would I see Dave doing to express that value? As I mentioned last week, it is one thing to have values, and it is another thing to live by them."

"Oops!" Dave replied. "I was just thinking too fast and getting ahead of myself. Yes, I have thought a lot about how one lives the value of family."

"I think you have to start with your own family. And it is really sorting out your priorities. As I said before, I was home a lot more for dinner this last week. And Sundays are family days in that we try to do something special together, maybe visit grandparents, or go to the zoo, or if nothing else, just eat out. But it is usually just the four of us."

"Another thing I have decided is to get more involved with what my children think is important, whether it is school or baseball or dance. I realized that Nancy and I—or really more I—have been focused on what we thought the kids would like, instead of asking them. In a sense I have been telling them what they should like dong. Some of that is okay in that it broadens their range of activities, but now we are going to do things together, but take their lead. As an example, my daughter keeps talking about getting into gymnastics and so we are looking for a place where she can start lessons."

"It looks like you thought a lot about your own family, but let's suppose you really got passionate about family values, how would that play out at work?" Rena asked. "Could you, or do you, have polices at work that support family values? What would those policies or practices look like?"

"Wow, you are really pushing me there," Dave replied. "I don't think I ever thought of family values in that context. I suppose I could say that we have great medical insurance benefits, and a few more things, but really I hadn't thought about it much. Can I take a temporary pass on that question?"

"No problem," Rena replied. "I was just pushing you a bit to think about how your values would play out in the broader context. For example, some companies are 'family friendly' in that they have programs and policies that benefit the families of their employees. Liberal maternity leave policies or even paternity leave would be examples of this. The point is that one needs to think of how to live one's values in a variety of settings. But let's put that discussion on hold and go on to your second value. You said it was education, wasn't it?"

"Education in the broadest sense," Dave replied. "Or maybe it is learning or self-improvement or something like that. Probably self-improvement is a better term. I think people have to keep learning and improving themselves. They can't get complacent and just coast. Things are always changing. Just look at the information technology revolution. Something new is coming out every day. And you have to keep on top of it, both as a business leader and as a person.

"The same is true of one's skills as a manager or a leader. You have to continuously change, to get better, to have a better understanding of your business, and a better understanding of your customers. Probably, most of all, you have to improve your leadership of people. That's the critical piece—leading people. That's where many leaders fail."

"How do I walk the walk on this one?" He continued, "Well, for one thing, I do set personal improvement goals periodically. For example, one goal is to become more computer literate. I spend about two hours each week with one of our IT people who briefs me on the latest software that we are using and also shows me how to use it.

"Another of my goals is to improve my presentation skills. I find that I am making more and more presentations each month. I use to just go into the meeting and rattle off some numbers. However, I realized that rattling off numbers is not very inspiring, particularly when you are talking to employees. So, I am working with one of our training people to improve both the content and delivery of my presentations.

"And still another goal is to work on my leadership skills. For some time I have been pretty uncomfortable with how I have been leading MMS, and have been looking around for some help. As you know I even thought of quitting MMS. But I am starting to see it isn't MMS, it is me. So a major goal is to refocus my efforts on myself and learn how to lead."

"Very good!" said Rena, "I can see that you do indeed walk the talk on this value. What's next?""

"Personal achievement or personal success is another top value of mine. I have always been an achiever. I always studied hard in school and was always in the top quarter of my class. I was never the brightest guy in the class, but I always applied myself.

"My mother had a bunch of sayings that she would spring on us kids. One of those was, 'It is not what you got, it's what you do with what you got!' She would always use that saying when we would complain that we were not terribly bright or very talented. That really stuck with me, and I have always thought that if you really apply yourself you can be successful, regardless of what talents you start with."

"Sounds like there are a couple of values here," said Rena. "One is that of personal achievement, and the other is of always doing the best you can. Maybe one is a goal and the other is a way to get to the goal?"

"You may have a point," answered Dave, "but in my mind they are lumped together. I had to work hard for most everything I achieved. For example, look at my brief sports career—I always wanted to be good and practiced hard, although, quite honestly, I didn't make the high school football team until my senior year. I didn't play in all of the games and was far from being a star. But the important point there is that I gave it my all. I never gave up, and I got great personal satisfaction from making the team and getting my athletic letter."

"Obviously, you carried that over to your business career, didn't you?" Rena interjected. "I remember hearing about your achievements at Kron."

"Right! When I was at Kron I always volunteered for the tough assignments, and loved the challenge. That's what helped me move up the ranks at the company. Kron really loved 'achievers.' They were quite open in saying that it was the achievers in the company that were the future of the company, and they had a policy of putting the achievers on the fast track, of moving them up the ladder quickly. So, I really fit in with their culture.

"You could argue that the top job at MMS was probably what I had been preparing for a long time at Kron, so when it came up, I jumped at the chance. It was hard to leave Kron, but this was my chance at the top job. So, I suppose the achievement and success value is very deeply ingrained in my psyche."

"But let me tell you about the other values," Dave continued. "Integrity is also at the top of my list. To me integrity means always being honest and truthful in all of your dealings with people. Never duck the truth even if it might be a bit painful.

"And integrity also means taking responsibility for your actions—if you say you are going to do something, do it! Once you make a commitment, follow through.

"When it comes down to it, integrity is all about trust. That is, can people trust you as a husband, a father, or even a CEO? People quickly spot a person who is a phony—a person who feeds them a lot of bull, and who doesn't follow through on commitments.

"I also think that integrity is one of those universal values that is understood and respected in different cultures and different situations. It is not only important in dealing with your family, but it is also critical in dealing with your employees and with your customers. Everyone wants to deal with someone who has integrity!"

"That's a great point," Rena commented. "If you look at the research that asked people in different countries what they saw as the most important value in their culture they usually said it was integrity, honesty, trust, or something like that. Some scholars think that in order to have a civilization you have to practice integrity, and it may be part of our genetic makeup. But before we get into bogged down in analyzing the genetic origin of our values, let's move on to the rest of your list."

Dave went on: "There is another value that I feel strongly about that is a new value for me. That is, it is a value that I probably would not have thought about a few years ago. That value is social responsibility. I really think that we all have to begin behaving in a more socially responsible way."

"Wow!" responded Rena. "That is a very large value. I mean you could talk about saving the rainforests, or saving whales, or stopping global warming, or the issues of labor abuses. Where do you start and where do you stop? How do you walk the walk on that value?"

"That's a great question," responded Dave, "and I really have thought a lot about it. My way of looking at social responsibility, or of being socially responsible, is to start by thinking about the impact of my actions or the company's actions on others as well as on the environment.

"For example, we recently formed a social responsibility committee at MMS. The committee has targeted several areas that we can do something about related to the environment or human rights. For example, we have a lot of overseas manufacturers that we didn't monitor much in the past except to make sure they shipped us a product that met our specifications.

"But now our committee has set some tough standards for all our manufacturers with regard to the environment and human rights. We joined an international organization whose membership consists of a group of U.S. companies with overseas suppliers. The organization actually audits overseas suppliers on a regular basis. And it has really made a difference. If these manufacturers don't meet the standards, they don't get our business.

"As you said, we can't save the whales but we can really do a lot by just looking at our own operations. That's my point regarding social responsibility. If everybody looked at what they do and how it impacts the environment or the human condition, we could make significant progress. That is true of businesses, and families, and individuals.

DAVE'S TOP LIFE VALUES

Family, Education or Self-Improvement, Personal Achievement, Integrity, and Social Responsibility

---

"Well, those are probably my top values. But I have a bunch more that are high on the list. For example, you may be surprised that religion is one of the values that is high on my list. For me, it really goes back to my childhood. I spent a lot of time in church, and in Sunday school, and most of the kids I hung around with growing up were in the church youth group with me. So religion, and a belief in God, has been part of my life as long as I can remember."

"I am not surprised at all," Rena answered. "There seem to be strong religious values, or sometimes it's called spirituality, in many of our top leaders."

"My religious values are not 'churchy,' if that makes sense," Dave continued. "I think they have more to do with moral principles than with church rules and regulations. I really think there are universal moral principles that people should live by, and every culture endorses these principles. It's the only way you can have a viable culture. Maybe it is tied to my value of integrity, and probably also has something to do with my recent interest in social responsibility. It is interesting how some values seem to be connected."

"Good observation," Rena remarked. "Many values for people seem to be related to each other. I don't think it is surprising since they are usually based on our experiences growing up and tend to organize them on a coherent whole.

"I can see you put a lot of thought into your values list." Rena continued, "This may sound like a stupid question, but bear with me. What did you learn from this exercise?"

"Oh, wow! This was a great exercise for me," Dave replied. "I reconnected with myself, if that makes any sense. It made me realize that I have some strong beliefs and strong values that are good in every sense of the word.

"I was having some doubts about myself, but this exercise forced me to go back and think about my background and my achievements, and quite frankly, I think Dave is a pretty good person, if I may say so myself.

"I came to the conclusion that I don't think I should be ashamed of who I am. I have the right values and the right background. What I need to do is really practice them—to keep my head high and to walk the walk."

"Great!" said Rena. "Now that you know who you are and what you value, let's push it a bit further and move on to leadership. I would like you to do a couple of things for next time. First, I want you to define leadership, especially effective leadership. What is leadership? And how would I know if a leader is effective? These are really critical questions that people, especially leaders, need to sort out.

"And let me emphasize, this has to be your definition of leadership. Not something you found in a book.

"Next, I want you to list your key leadership values. What do you see as the most important values of leadership? And remember, they have to be your values, not something you found in a leadership manual. In fact, you are prohibited from looking at another source, such as a book, or even talking to someone. These have to be Dave's values. And further, I want you to explain how one would walk the walk on your leadership values—what would I see someone doing if they were exercising the values?"

"Ah, I do have a question about leadership values. Should my leadership values be specific to leadership? Or are they more general values that can be applied in a lot of situations? Am I making myself clear?" Dave asked.

"I think I know where you are going with that, and it is an interesting question," Rena replied, "but I am going to let you figure that out.

"However, I would add that your values should support each other. People who live by a system of values that support one another are most effective. For example, you can't be a dictator and also believe in collaboration. Those two ideas or values just do not fit together.

"And I suggest we meet in two weeks for this. I want to give you a little time to think about the assignment. Does that make sense?"

"Makes sense to me," Dave responded. "Actually, it sounds like two very important questions that I probably thought about from time to time, but not to the extent that I put something down in writing. It sounds like I am ready to do that.

"I also want to tell you that I am beginning to understand what this is all about. It is all coming together. Talking with you and doing these exercises has really been helpful. I just want you to know that it is working, and I appreciate your help."

"Thank you for the kind words," Rena replied. "But you are a great learner and that is the critical part. You are doing the work, and I am just providing some direction. The important question in my business is whether the learner is ready to learn. You are ready, and I am very optimistic about your future."

With that exchange they said their goodbyes.

HOMEWORK ASSIGNMENT

What Is Leadership?

What is your definition of effective leadership? What are some of the most important responsibilities of a leader? What do effective leaders do that distinguishes them from leaders that are not effective?

HOMEWORK ASSIGNMENT

What Are Your Leadership Values?

What do you see as the most important values of leadership? These have to be your values, not something you read in a book.

If you were practicing these values to their fullest, what would we see you doing? That is, how would a person "walk the talk" on these values?

6

Now What Are Your Leadership Values?

The two weeks went by quickly. Dave spent much of his time prepping for an analysts' meeting in New York. MMS was thinking of raising some cash, probably through a stock offering, but they first wanted to test the waters to see what the financial people thought of the company.

Dave also noticed that he was spending more time with the family. The kids are growing up, he thought, and I don't want to miss these years with them.

However, he also had spent a lot of time thinking about the questions that Rena had posed, particularly about his leadership values, and was eager to start talking about them.

Dave wasted no time once he got to Rena's office. "Want to hear my definition of leadership?" he asked as soon as they were seated.

"Let's go!" Rena replied. "You seem all fired up!"

"I am fired up," Dave agreed. "I have been thinking about this for two weeks, and I probably went through 15 definitions. Here is the latest—

Becoming a Values-Based Leader, pages 41–53
41

'Leaders are people who help groups or organizations move to a higher level of success or effectiveness.' That's the short form.

"To elaborate, leaders bring people together, and help them define their goals and then help them accomplish those goals. You asked about effective leaders—well, I think a leader is effective if the group or the organization achieves their goals. So the criterion of leader effectiveness is not the leader, but what happens to the group. Does the group move in the desired direction? The group may not be totally successful because there are a lot of factors that cannot be controlled. But did they create a vision and a plan and an organization that moved them ahead?"

DAVE'S DEFINITION OF LEADERSHIP

Leaders are people who help groups or organizations move to a higher level of success or effectiveness.

"Wait, wait," Rena interrupted. "I have a couple of questions. You seem to be rejecting the heroic leadership model: the model in which some great person stands up and says follow me and do what I say and we will conquer all. Am I correct?"

"You are absolutely correct," Dave responded. "That heroic stuff only works in the movies. Effective leaders involve others in the organization to develop the direction for the organization. In that way, the other people become committed to the goals, and better still, the organization has a better chance of success because you are using the collective expertise of the organization.

"Occasionally, you read in the newspaper that some CEO turned a company around. Somebody became the CEO of a failing company and three years later the company was making money, and therefore the CEO is heralded as a business hero. But what happened to the 3,000 other people in the company? Without their involvement and commitment nothing would have happened."

"But aren't you absolving the leader from making decisions?" Rena countered. "Aren't you putting the responsibility on other people?"

"Not at all," Dave responded. "Leaders are responsible for focusing on the important questions and issues in an organization or group, and keeping the organization focused on those issues. And while leaders may get a lot of input from others, many decisions are not that clear cut, and the correct path may not be obvious to all. It's the leader's job to make the final decision and it often takes a lot of courage."

"I take it that you are an advocate of the distributive approach to leadership, which argues that the entire organization should be loaded with leaders?" Rena asked.

"Absolutely," Dave said. "In my definition of leadership, everyone in the organization can be a leader. In fact, I think that in order for an organization to be successful, they have to have leadership throughout the organization. Leadership means jumping in and identifying problems or issues, and moving the unit toward resolving the issues. It has to happen at all levels and all units of the organization.

"And that leads me into my top leadership values. Are you ready for them?"

"Great," said Rena. "Keep going—you are really on a roll!"

"Well, first let me answer the question I asked you a couple of weeks ago about leadership values. I think leadership values should be specific to leadership. That is, going back to my definition of leadership, one's leadership values should create successful organizations. If you walk the walk on your leadership values, your group or your organization will be effective and successful. It is almost like a philosophy of leadership—your leadership values should be your rules or principles for creating successful organizations.

"And different people will have different leadership values. My leadership values are probably not the same as Charlie Schaefer's values. However, I do think that there are some values that all leaders must have. For example, having integrity is a key value for leaders. Otherwise no one will trust you and your leadership will be short-lived."

"But how do your life values and life purpose fit into all this?" asked Rena.

"I thought about that also," Dave responded. "I think your life values and your purpose are the foundation for living a fulfilling and happy life. That is, if you live your life according to your purpose and values, you will be very happy. On the other hand, if you don't live your life according to your values or purpose, you will probably be unhappy or at least feel that something is missing. So, while your leadership values are specific to leadership, they should be an extension of your life values. In that way your life can be fulfilling—you are living your values. Does that make sense?"

"Good points! You have really thought this out," Rena said, "but now I am eager to hear about your leadership values."

"Well, let me first say that I divided my leadership values into two parts. The first part is character values, and the second part is leadership values. In my mind if a person doesn't have character, no one will follow, so character values come first. Character is the foundation for leadership, and there are several values that make up character."

"That's an interesting way to look at it," Rena said, "So, tell me about character."

"For starters, my number one character value is integrity," Dave went on. "As I noted before, you cannot be a leader without integrity; it's that fundamental. Integrity is the basis for leadership. No one will follow your lead or even listen to you if you don't have integrity. I think it is the basis for—if you don't have integrity, no one will trust you.

"I initially called this first value trust, or better yet, developing trust. But then I realized that if people trust you it is because you earned it, and the way to earn it is through integrity and respect and several other values. So, I changed my number one value to integrity."

"Good logic, and a great first value," Rena responded. "But what does it mean? What does a person with integrity do? How does a person show integrity?"

"Aha!" said Dave. "I knew you would ask me that. Great question!

"I think integrity has several components. One of those is honesty. A leader has to be honest with everyone. That means always telling the truth. Sometimes the truth isn't pretty and it may hurt, but you can't lie to people and you can't be evasive. You have to tell it like it is.

"Related to honesty is the sharing of information and opinions. You have to let people know what is going on. You can't hide things from people, and very importantly, you don't play games with people!

"And a third point—integrity means being true to your word. If you say you will do something, then do it! Maybe that is more like being responsible, but I think that it fits into the integrity category.

"I think I do pretty well on the integrity value in that I try to communicate with all employees and customers through our newsletters and meetings. And I make sure I follow up on any promise I make. The honesty part is a bit tougher. For example, I met last week with one of our production people who wants to be running our manufacturing in the Far East. He is a good technical person, but he really seems to irritate people. We can't afford to put him in that position. So, how do you tell him that?"

"Well, did you tell him?" asked Rena.

"No, I didn't," answered Dave. "He never asked me for a decision or an evaluation, but he simply wanted to let me know he was interested in the position. But at some point, probably soon, we are going to have to be honest with him. I think we have been avoiding that discussion because we like his technical skills and want to keep him at MMS. Those are the really tough discussions that I think we tend to avoid."

"As a side issue, what type of discussion would you have with him? What would that discussion be all about?" Rena asked.

"Well, in general, it should be developmental in that we would try to help him develop his skills so that he would be able to be successful at a higher level position," replied Dave. "I would start out talking about his strengths and then move into the areas in which he needs to improve. We would probably end with deciding on a development plan that would improve those areas in which he is having problems."

"Very nice! Those tough discussions are much easier when they are taken in a development context in which the person is given some help correcting his or her difficulties," Rena said, "but let's move on with your values list."

"My second value is treating everyone with fairness and respect. That's another thing that people want. They want to know that you respect their opinions and respect them, and you have to show it! And fairness comes with that. People want to be treated fairly. No favoritism, no old boy network.

"Let me tell you a good example of applying that value. Prior to my coming to MMS, promotions and assignments were a mystery. That is, people didn't know why or how people were promoted or assigned to jobs at MMS, and they were very unhappy about the process. We changed that a couple of years ago and now all position openings are publically posted, as are the criteria for the job. We tried to make promotions and assignments as fair and open as possible, and employees are much more satisfied with the process.

"As to respect, I think just valuing others' ideas and opinions is a big factor here. We instituted a general rule at MMS that 'the idea is more important than the person who made it.' The rule means that is we should seriously consider everyone's ideas, regardless of their position in the organization. This has really led to a lot of improvements that we would not have made if we just considered who offered the idea rather than what the idea was."

"Those are good examples on how to walk the walk," Rena responded. "You have to make values real and relevant to everyday life otherwise they are meaningless. I like your examples, but let's move to your next value."

"Value number three is to strive for excellence in everything that you do. This is a more personal value that I probably learned from my father and my football coach. Can I tell you a story?"

"Please do," said Rena.

"This whole excellence thing really struck me several years ago when I was getting my MBA. I had a couple of years of experience under my belt and my boss at Kron encouraged me to get the MBA, and the company was nice enough to pay the tuition.

"In a lot of the classes we were put in teams and assigned a project. One thing I quickly noticed about the teams is that some team members, such as me, really wanted to do a great job on the project. But there were others who just wanted to do the minimum effort to get a passing grade.

"That really shocked me. Here are people paying big money for their MBA and their goal is to just get by. Unbelievable! And why would a company hire someone with that attitude?

"I swore that I would never be like that group of people—I would always strive for excellence regardless of the assignment. And furthermore, I would never tolerate that just-get-by attitude from my direct reports. So, I always strive for excellence in my work and, very importantly, expect the same from others.

"After I finish a project or make a decision I always ask myself if I did my best on it, and if I haven't, I will keep at it. For example, I just finished the presentation I will make to the financial analysts in New York. My financial people and I must have reworked it ten times, because I want the analysts to be impressed with MMS. I could have quit with version three, which would have been quite adequate, but it would not have been my best."

"On the surface this is a very simple value," Rena said, "but it has broad consequences, doesn't it? It leads to much better outcomes and many fewer problems down the line."

"That's true," Dave agreed. "The way to avoid problems is to do it right in the first place.

"Courage is my personal character value number four. I want to be able to have the courage to make the tough decisions that a leader has to make. I also want the courage to always take the high road, and the ethical road, no matter what the situation is. Another part of this value for me is the courage to trust others, particularly my direct reports. Sometimes, that is tough. And sometimes it takes a lot of courage to be honest with people as we were just discussing regarding my production person.

"I think it is sometimes a lot easier for a leader not to face reality or not to deal with problems squarely. I know that when problems arise I often think that if I don't do anything maybe they will go away. Or sometimes I have tried to please everyone and ended up pleasing no one. But that is not what a leader should do, and it doesn't work anyway. I have found out that not having the courage to make the correct decision just leads to more problems."

"Some people think courage also applies to the self-examination we are doing here, don't you think?" Rena asked.

"It is probably a lot broader than simply what we are doing here. It is having the courage to be honest with myself—to look at myself or to get feedback about myself and not get defensive. I often find myself getting defensive when someone offers what might be a legitimate criticism. Another tough thing to do is to change when it is obvious that I have to change. Now that really takes courage. However, I do find that working with you seems to help me change much more easily, although I am not sure why."

"It is probably because you are in charge of the change," replied Rena. "You are discovering where you want to go in your development. I am not telling you what you need to change, you are discovering it. That makes change much easier. But let's move on."

"Well, those are the four values that I call the character values—integrity, fairness and respect, striving for excellence, and courage." Dave continued, "Do you want to hear the other part of the values equation—the leadership values?"

"I sure do," Rena replied. "And I'm extremely impressed with what you have said so far. You really thought this out. Keep talking."

"Well, my first leadership value is simply 'to lead.' I know this might sound a little vague but hear me out on this.

"All the good leaders I worked for, as well as those in history—for example, Martin Luther King—provided a sense of direction, a focus, or a vision. They didn't say, gee, I don't know where we should go, so everybody just do their thing. Rather they said very clearly this is what we have to do to be good, or be the best, or to be free. They established a clear vision or direction for the organization or the movement and worked hard on getting everybody on the same page, focusing on the same objectives, and working together on the same goals.

"I don't mean that these leaders were dictators. Often they had a lot of help in deciding the best direction for the organization. But once that direction was established it was their responsibility to talk it, to walk it, and to sell it. That is what leading is all about.

"If I were to look at all of my values and to give myself a rating on each, this would be the one on which I probably would score myself low. I remember Charlie Schaefer yelling at me a couple of months ago when told him that my role at MMS was that of 'chief problem solver.' He was pretty blunt and said that that wasn't my role, and that my role was 'to lead.' So, of all the values, this is the one I need to work on. Actually, if I had led much more strongly I would have had a lot fewer problems to solve."

"I remember you telling me about Charlie Schaefer's comment on leadership when we first met," said Rena, "and my impression is that you have made a lot of progress moving from a problem solver to a leader. But leaders also do have to solve problems don't they?"

"No question about that," replied Dave. "Some of the tougher questions end up in your lap. Those are the questions that can't be resolved anyplace else in the organization. But even then you need to have a great deal of input from your key people—which, by the way, leads me to my next leader value.

"My second leader value is to involve, develop and empower your people. This means getting people involved in the decisions, getting their input, letting them research the issue, and listening to what they have to say. Someone said that you should only hire people who are brighter than yourself in a particular area, otherwise why hire them? If you hire the most talented people you can find, let them show their talent.

"And the 'empower' part says that you should trust them, just as you want them to trust you. Give them the responsibility and the authority to make the decisions in their areas of expertise. That was the mistake I made with Red and Anita. I should never have let Red go above Anita's head. She is really a brilliant marketing leader, and I should have trusted her to handle Red. That doesn't mean you can't question their decision and have a dialogue with them about some issues—that's just good business. But it means that you let them run their department without your interference.

"One of the interesting aspects of empowerment is that it leads to employee development. Some people think employee development is about sending employees to training seminars. That is not true—employee development, or at least good employee development, is involving and empowering them to sort through problems and make decisions on their own. Working with Charlie Schaefer at Kron made me really think about this value. He empowered people, and they learned to lead, and they really delivered for Kron. So, to me, empowerment is the key for developing an organization loaded with leaders."

"So, how are you doing on that value?" asked Rena.

"Much better," laughed Dave. "As an example, I had a long talk with Anita, and apologized for my behavior, and now she is directly dealing with Red as well as the people at Hathorn Medical Systems. And I might add she is doing a much better job at it than I did."

"Embracing change is my next leader value," Dave continued. "MMS has to keep getting better; it has got to keep changing to provide better products and better service. I don't think I did that in the past at MMS. I have been too willing to keep doing the same thing, and hoping for different results. The people who started MMS were innovators, but now we seem to be followers. We need to keep innovating, worrying less about keeping up with our competitors, and focusing more on providing extraordinary value for the customer. That's what leading businesses do. That's what we have to do!"

"Isn't this more of an organization value or a company value, rather than a leadership value?" Rena asked.

"I think it is both," answered Dave. "MMS has to embrace change, but as a leader I have to push change. I don't mean change for the sake of change. I mean the type of change that will make us a more viable company. To give you a good example, in the next few years the major companies in our industry will be global companies. If MMS wants to be one of the major players, we will have to become a global company, and that means big changes for MMS. My point is that MMS needs to change, but to do so it needs a leader who is a change leader, not someone who is comfortable with the status quo."

"I see where you are going with that value," Rita said. "If I were looking to hire an executive for a dynamic company, I certainly would be looking for someone who is both comfortable and experienced in leading change."

"My last value is related to change and may surprise you a bit—it is to focus on results. You probably would think that all businesses focus on results, but they really don't. Sometimes they put too much focus on process, and not on outcomes. Is R&D coming out with new products? Is manufacturing purchasing new equipment? Are the salespeople making their contacts? All of these things are important, but what is most important is what do your sales and profits look like?

"It is my greatest desire to create a company in which the employees are treated with respect and dignity, enjoy their work, have great pay and benefits, have opportunities for advancement, and pretty well know that the company will have continued success and they will have a future in the company. And we want to have a company that gives back in some way to the community. But in order to do all of this the company has to make some solid profits. Without some solid profits, all of these other very important activities and practices would be impossible.

"I realize that it sounds like I am on a soap box for capitalistic profit making, but I firmly believe that it is very important. When MMS began several years ago, the company couldn't afford health insurance and so the company didn't provide any. However, now MMS has one of the best health insurance plans in the industry, and it is because we can afford it.

"We also recently began paying for the auditing of our suppliers in third world companies to insure that they have humane labor practices. We don't have to do that, and whether we do it or not probably has no effect on our bottom line because people who buy medical supplies don't ask those questions. But we think it is the socially responsible thing to do, and we can do it is because we have the financial resources to do it. That's my point."

"But why is this a leader value?" Rena asked. "Would this apply to someone in the ministry?"

"Profits may not be a leader value for everyone—for example, for someone in the civil rights movement or in the military," Dave replied, "but I would argue they should be results oriented, and let them decide what results are important for the mission of their organization.

"On the other hand, I believe leadership values are very personal. If someone else came up with a list of eight or ten leadership values, it probably would be different than my list. I don't mean to impose my values on others. I am just saying that these are my important leader values."

"Good point! Values are personal," Rena replied. "However, I do think that many of the values on your list would show up on the lists of most people. As you pointed out at the beginning of this session, leader values should lead to organization success. And there are some values that most leaders would agree are necessary for organizational success. Speaking of necessary values, do you have other values on your list?"

"No, that's it. My character values are to have integrity, to show fairness and respect, to always strive for excellence, and to have courage. And my leader values are to lead, to empower and develop, to embrace change, and to focus on results.

"I limited my values to eight, because I think values are like goals. If you have 20 goals, none of them will get accomplished. If you have six or eight goals, they all will be accomplished. It's the same with values. You have to decide the few that are really important and then live by them. And these are the eight I want to live by.

"And again I want to emphasize that these are my leadership values and someone else would probably come up with a different list. So what do you think?"

DAVE'S LEADERSHIP VALUES

Integrity; Fairness and Respect; Striving for Excellence; Courage; Leading, Involving, Developing, and Empowering Employees; Embracing Change; and Focusing on Results

"Wow! I am really impressed. You really took this seriously," Rena responded. "I am really impressed with the thought you put into your values, and the reasons you decided to focus only on eight. I don't really know what to say, except to say that you did a great job! Congratulations!"

"Thank you for the compliment," Dave replied. "And I also want to thank you for leading me through the exercise. This really helped me sort out a lot of things. It particularly helped me sort out what it means to be a leader, and also clarified my leadership role as the CEO of MMS. It is very clear to me now what I have to do to be an effective leader."

"You are most welcome," Rena replied. "That's what coaches do—bring out the talent in others. It's very much like your value of Involvement and Empowerment and Development of Others."

"So, what's next?" Dave asked. "Did I finish the course?"

"The course is not quite over," Rena laughed. "But you are getting an A so far, maybe even an A+. Actually, you just finished the easy part. The next part is the really tough part. Do you want to guess what it is?"

"Oh, I know!" said Dave. "The next step is about implementing the values. It is about walking the walk, isn't it? Now I have to execute."

"Perfect, right on," replied Rena. "A lot of people have values statements, and a lot of companies have a values statement that get posted somewhere, but are never enacted. Those values are just a bunch of hot air—a waste of the paper they are printed on. And it's pretty hypocritical or phony because they say they will behave in one way, but actually do something different.

"So your next assignment is to decide how you are going to walk the talk. How are you going to actually implement your values?"

"Do you have any suggestions?" Dave asked.

"I do, but I am not going to give them to you," Rena replied. "And my reason is very simple—you are doing a great job sorting things out without my advice, and I am convinced that you will do an excellent job on deciding how to implement your values without my advice.

"I would urge you to think about this carefully," she continued. "One mistake managers make is that they suddenly change their behavior and it catches people off guard. Employees get confused. One day the manager behaves in one way, and the next day the manager is behaving very differently. People don't know what to make of that.

"Another consideration is whether your expectations for others are also going to change. You defined *your* leadership values, but are you also going to hold others, for example, your key associates, to those same values? If so, how will they know the standards have changed?"

"Great points," replied Dave. "I can see this isn't going to be easy."

Dave stood by the door silently for a moment or two thinking about what to do. Then he caught himself and said, "Right. I have a lot to think about, don't I? Should I see you again in a couple of weeks?"

"I am not sure we need to meet again," Rena quickly replied. "I think you have done a great job at sorting things out. I think you are now clear as to who you are, and where you are going, and what you need to do to get there. Why don't we leave the next appointment open? If you think you need help, give me a call. However, sometime down the line I would like to get together again to see how your approach to leadership is working."

"Got it!" Dave replied. "Many, many thanks for your help. And yes, I will get back to you to tell you how it all worked out."

As Dave was walking out the door Rena called to him: "Hey, you forgot to ask me what to do about Red. You ask me that every time we meet, don't you?"

Dave let out a big laugh and said, "No, I am not going to ask you about Red ever again. As you have told me repeatedly, this isn't about Red, it's about Dave. And now that I am beginning to understand Dave, I don't have to ask you about Red."

On his way home, Dave started to think about how he was going to walk the walk. The first step, he thought, was to somehow inform his management team of the changes in his leadership approach. But how to do that?

As he thought about it, the way to do it seemed obvious. My number one value is integrity, he said to himself, which means being open and honest with everyone. So, if I am going to follow my values, I will have to just lay it out, just tell people about my journey and what I discovered, and what changes I want to make to my leadership approach.

Now that he decided on the how, the next question was when. Dave thought he had the ideal time.

HOMEWORK ASSIGNMENT

Communicating Your Values

How would you communicate your life values, and/or your leadership values, to your associates (or your family)?

7

Monday Morning with the "Veep Squad"

The executive team at MMS is jokingly called the "Veep Squad," as it consists of the vice presidents of all the major functions at MMS plus a few of the associate vice presidents. They get together every Monday morning, and while everyone is expected to make a brief report, the meeting is usually dominated by the leaders in finance, marketing and sales, and manufacturing. However, Dave had notified the group that the agenda for this Monday's meeting would be different, although he did not specify how it would be different.

Coffee, rolls, and juice are served in the conference room at 7:15, and the meeting begins precisely at 8:00 a.m. Most of the team arrives early, and the room is usually filled with a lot of noisy chatter and joking, particularly about whose favorite baseball team won or last the day before.

At 8:00 Dave began the meeting by saying that they would not follow the typical agenda this morning because he wanted to share some recent personal experiences with them. He continued, "I am not exactly sure how to talk about this other than to just lay it out and be honest with you about what I have been going through the last few months."

Becoming a Values-Based Leader, pages 55–62
Copyright © 2012 by Information Age Publishing
All rights of reproduction in any form reserved.

With that, the room became deadly silent.

"As some of you are aware, I have not been happy with my stay at MMS, particularly in the last year." He went on, "So, I sought some counsel from an old friend who referred me to an executive coach. I will not go through all of the details, except to say that I soon realized that my problem had nothing to do with MMS, but rather had a lot to do with me, Dave.

"I think the best way to explain all of this is to briefly go through what I did and what I found out about what I want to be," he continued.

Dave then talked about his work with Rena, and how he first identified the people who most influenced him as well as what he learned from them. He then talked about identifying his purpose in life, as well as his life values and what they were.

The room was quiet.

"All of this is a prelude to what I really want to talk to you about today, which are my leadership values," he continued. "And the reason I want to share these with you is that this is the way I think I should lead, these are the values I want to follow as the CEO of MMS, these are the behaviors you can expect from me, and I expect you to hold me accountable for walking the walk on these values."

With that introduction, he went over to a flip chart and wrote the words "Leadership'" and "Values."

"First, let me define leadership. I think leadership is helping groups or organizations move to a higher level of success or effectiveness. So, the criterion for leadership is whether the group or organization moves ahead, overcomes problems, achieves its goals, or whatever the organization needs to do to become more effective.

DAVE'S DEFINITION OF LEADERSHIP

Leaders are people who help groups or organizations move to a higher level of success or effectiveness.

"I think one of my big problems as a leader at MMS is that I bought into the theory that I was 'the chief problem solver' of the organization, and was here to solve the major problems of the organization. But that is not leadership. Leaders have to develop a sense of direction for the organization, including goals and a strategy, and things like that.

"And they have to do it in collaboration with the people in the organization. Leadership should not be a power trip for the CEO! It is not about me, it is about *we*. It is about all of us working together to make MMS a success."

The room remained silent.

"So, how do we, or rather I, implement this way of leading? Well, I think the best way to do it is through the exercise of values. And I have come up with eight leadership values that I think nicely outline how I would like to lead. These are the values that I intend to follow, and these are the values that I would like you to hold me accountable.

"The first couple of my values are really character values, and character value number one is Integrity," he began. He further explained that in his mind, a person who walked the walk on integrity would be open and honest with everyone—that is, he would always tell the truth even if the truth is unpleasant, and he wouldn't hide things from people, nor have any hidden agendas. Moreover, a person who practices integrity would always be true to his or her word. If they say they will do something, it will get done.

Now the room started to come alive. The "Veep Squad" could see where this was going and started to pitch in with suggestions, including the suggestion that everyone at MMS should practice, and be held accountable, for practicing integrity.

"Hold on," Dave said, "let me finish and then we can have a discussion."

DAVE'S LEADERSHIP VALUES

Integrity; Fairness and Respect; Striving for Excellence; Courage; To Lead; To Involve, Develop, and Empower Employees; To Embrace Change; and To Focus on Results

---

He then went through the values of respect and fairness, and striving for excellence, and having courage to make the correct decisions.

"Those four values are what I have called character values, and my next four are what I call my leadership values," Dave continued. As soon as he announced that his first value in this category was "To Lead" the Veep Group again burst out with comments and suggestions. It seemed that everyone had an idea as to what it means "to lead."

Dave kept trying to get control of the meeting, and finally was able to briefly outline his remaining values—to involve and empower, to embrace change, and finally to focus on results.

After he finished, Dave again emphasized that these were his values and other people may come up with other values, but that these were his, and these are the values that he wants to practice from now on at MMS. Moreover, he wants to be held accountable by the "Veep Squad" for walking the walk on these values.

Dar Shah, the VP for Finance, asked for the floor so he could "show the group something important." Dar is usually a very quiet person and rarely speaks unless called upon to do so. But today he seemed excited about talking about values. He said that his family in India had a "values crest," which was used to present the values that were practiced by his family. Then he started talking about Mahatma Gandhi and how Gandhi was a great leader who helped free India from British rule, and how Gandhi was a person who lived by his values and never wavered from his goal or his values.

"Here is how I see your values, Dave," he continued as he went to the flip chart. "I think you have four character values and four leadership values—it's four times four. Character values relate to whether people can trust you and respect your ideas, and leadership values are whether you have the capability to lead those who trust you."

He then put a 2 × 2 matrix on the flip chart, with character values on one dimension and leadership values on the other, each ranging from low to high (Figure 7.1). Dar pointed to the lower left hand square and said that the people who fall in that square are people who are both low on leadership and low on character. "Keep away from those people," he added. "They can't be trusted and they can't lead. They are just a lot of hot air."

He continued by pointing to the box in the upper left hand square. "These are people who have solid leadership values but are low on charac-

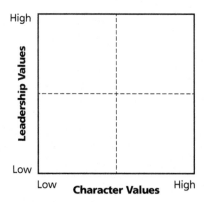

Figure 7.1   Dar's leadership values model.

ter values. They know how to lead and know how to involve and develop people, but they can't be trusted. You might follow their lead," Dar said, "but watch them closely. You are probably going to end up very disappointed, as these people are out for themselves; they are not out for you or for the company."

Redbeard the Pirate's name suddenly came into Dave's head. Red would probably fit in that square. He did have some leadership skills in that he was good at getting his staff focused and trained on making sales. However, Red's leadership values are a bit different from mine, Dave thought. Red's problem is that he plays loose and fast with the rules. Bottom line was that you can't trust Red. Actually, Dar's description of the people in that upper left square fit Red almost exactly; however, Dave was not about to jump up and proclaim that revelation.

Dar continued, "This lower right hand square consists of people who are high in character but low on leadership. Great people," he said. "That is, great people to work with, but they haven't learned how to lead. So, this is not a person that you want to put in charge of a project, because the results are likely to be disappointing."

Dar's description of the people in this square also struck a chord with Dave. MMS had a bunch of employees like those. Very solid people, very good workers, but they were somehow unable to play a leadership role. We need to work with this group, Dave thought. This group of people could really make a much stronger contribution to MMS if we could just develop some of their leadership abilities.

"However, in upper right hand box are people who have character— people you can trust, and who also can lead. These are the people that you want to follow. This is the box that Gandhis of the world are in. This is the box of all the great leaders." Dar continued, speaking very seriously, "Dave, if you can move into this box you will be a great leader for MMS."

With that the Veep Squad broke into applause and cheers for Dar's presentation, and also for Dave.

Once the group settled down Dave said, "I am not sure what I can say after that. Beautiful presentation, Dar, and I do agree with your ideas. Leaders do have to have character in order for anyone to trust them, but they also have to lead. Your model illustrates this very nicely, and yes, I hope with the help of all of you, I can move into the upper right-hand box!"

Again, the Veep Squad broke into applause.

"Wait, I have something else to say," Dar said, waving his arms. "A point I wanted to emphasize is that these values all make a contribution to creating an effective organization. That is, each value adds something, and if you are missing a couple of values, then the whole system won't work. They are all connected in a value system, and you need to implement the package to make it work. Do you understand what I am saying?"

"I understand your model," said Michael, the VP of Manufacturing, "but I need a practical example. You said that one of your heroes was Gandhi. Does Gandhi fit in your model?"

"Yes, Gandhi fits the model perfectly." answered Dar. "Let me explain. Gandhi certainly had character. You could trust whatever he said. And he had compassion for the people of India, and also for the British, by the way. He showed respect for all people. And he had unbelievable courage."

"But he also led! He provided a clear sense of direction and goal—freedom for the people of India. And also a method for achieving that goal—that of nonviolence. He motivated the people of India, and involved others, and embraced change. That's the leadership part." Then Dar pointed to the upper right had quadrant of the model on the flip chart, "He, Gandhi, is clearly in this box, which is the box of great leaders."

"Wow!" said Dave, "I had not thought about leadership values, and my leadership values in that way. The model makes sense, but I am going to have to think about it a bit more before I jump on your band wagon."

"I'm with Dar," said Michael, "maybe not in all of the details, but I like Dar's premise that says that leaders have to be strong on character values and leadership values in order to be effective. I think that's what leading with values is all about. And yes, you have to implement the total package to make it work! You can't pick and choose what you want to do.

"Moreover, that's what has been missing at MMS!" Michael continued. "We have a vision statement and a company values statement, but what is missing is a statement on how we should manage or how we should lead. Different people have different philosophies, and we are not all on the same page. That's what we need to move MMS ahead, a philosophy that we all adhere to!"

"I agree," jumped in Anita, "we really need something that tells us how to run the company. I agree with Dar, it's a value system. It is a set of interrelated values, each of which contributes to effective leadership and to company success, but a person has to implement the entire system to maximize effectiveness.

"And let me share an insight I just had regarding our ethics problems with Redbeard and others. I think our problem is that we try to enforce ethics as an independent issue, something not related to the other things we do. That is the big problem that we, and other people, make in thinking about ethics. If we had a coherent values system that everyone adhered to, most of our ethics problems would disappear. People with a solid and coherent value system don't have to go to our Web site to see what is ethical and what is not."

That comment brought a variety of suggestions, including one person who wanted everyone in the company to adopt Dave's eight values, and another who suggested that each member of the Veep Squad develop their own set of values.

"Wait, wait!" said Dave. "My reason for starting this presentation was to tell you about my journey over the past few weeks and how I rediscovered my purpose and values, as well as my motivation to lead. It was really to help you better understand me, Dave. I didn't intend to push my values on others. I think that each of you has to discover what is important to you, and discover your own leadership values. Don't take my values or the values of anyone else!"

"I think we all understand your point," Dar replied. "This has been a very profitable discussion, and I think what is coming out of it is that everyone needs to examine their own purpose and values.

"But, in addition, we are also saying is that MMS needs to have a consistent leadership philosophy or approach so that everybody is on the same page. And in my mind, it means agreeing on a set of values, both character values and leadership values, that we hold everyone to."

"Let me play the devil's advocate here." said Dave. "Suppose I come up with a purpose and a set of values that I feel very strongly about, and MMS develops a set of values that they want all leaders, or all employees to adhere to. What if my values conflict with the values of MMS? What happens then?"

"Great question!" Anita answered. "If your values conflict with the MMS values then there isn't a fit! And you probably would not be happy at MMS. But look at it this way. We would know if there was a fit or not. Right now we haven't endorsed any set of values, and we get frustrated when we are dealing with employees who obviously live by a different set of values than ours. We have a prime example of that in my sales area.

"So, I agree with Dar. I think people, if they are so inclined, should discover or rediscover their purpose and values. I think that is very important, and I for one, am going to go through the same process as you just went through Dave. But we also need to take a values approach to leadership at MMS and outline a set of leader values that we expect all employees to adhere to. Moreover, these values should be well thought out such that they will, if followed, lead to the success of MMS.

"I think values-based leaders should create values-based organizations. And the way to do that is for everybody to sort out their values, but also for the company to decide what values they want their leaders to lead by."

Again, the group broke into a round of applause.

"I am getting the message," Dave said, "and I think I understand where we need to go with this. First, I am suggesting that we set up a process by which anyone who wants to can go through the process of discovering their purpose and values. Maybe we can contact my coach, Rena, and have her available to lead people through the process. That would be strictly on a volunteer basis.

"The other action would be the development of a list of values that we would expect all leaders, indeed all employees, to adhere to at MMS. They would have to walk the walk on these values. It could follow the model that Dar proposed with a set of character values and a set of leadership values. Together the two sets would form the MMS leadership model much like the 2×2 matrix that Dar put on the flip chart. I don't know if that is the best way to formulate the MMS values, but it is certainly something we could start with.

"We really covered a lot of ground today. Quite frankly, I really didn't know how you would react to my telling you about my values search. But I am pleased how it came out. Given the time, and the importance of this topic, let me suggest that we defer our discussion on this until next Monday, and I would urge you to think about this issue and be prepared to discuss it in more detail then. I suspect the best way to go would be to form a committee on Monday who can take your ideas and come up with a proposed list. Does that make sense?"

His question was followed by another round of applause.

With that Dave adjourned the meeting, noting this was the most applause he had received at any of the Veep Squad meeting—"So, we must be on to something important."

8

Another One of Charlie Schaefer's Barbeques

Charlie Schaefer had left messages for Dave several times during the weeks leading up to Halloween to invite Dave and Nancy for what he called "the last official barbeque of the season." "I am not taking no for an answer," Charlie kept saying, and Dave assumed that Charlie was very curious as to how he was making out at MMS, since they had not been in contact for a couple of months. So, Dave promised he would be there.

When he and Nancy arrived at Charlie's place, he was surprised that they were the only couple invited, although the more he thought about it, the more he realized that Charlie had probably arranged this little get-together to get an update from him. It was a little cool on the patio; however, the food was delicious as usual. Ribs, corn on the cob, a couple of salads, and homemade cherry pie for dessert.

Charlie seemed antsy to be alone with Dave, and shortly after dessert was served he asked to be excused and that he and Dave as they had some business to discuss. With that he asked Dave to join him in his den.

Becoming a Values-Based Leader, pages 63–69
Copyright © 2012 by Information Age Publishing
All rights of reproduction in any form reserved.

"What the heck has been going on with you?" Charlie began, "I haven't heard from you and I am dying of curiosity! What happened with Rena? You did call and told me that things were going well with her, but I didn't hear the outcome. Are you leaving MMS? What is happening with your career?"

"Sorry, I haven't kept you on the loop," replied Dave, "but things have been so hectic in the last few months that I haven't had time to talk to anyone.

"To answer your question, yes, I am still at MMS, and quite frankly I am having a ball. The company has a new vision and a new strategy, and we rolled out several new products, moved into South America, did some restructuring, and were successful at a new stock offering. Actually we are on a roll—things could not be better. And to give credit where credit is due, it all started with my conversation with you, and I owe you a great deal for that."

"You are welcome, but I don't think I did that much. But tell me about your visits with Rena," Charlie said.

"Rena was great! What I learned from her was that I needed to reconnect with my values and beliefs. She made me think about myself—who I am, where I came from, and what my values are. Once I got that straight, the rest was easy!" Dave explained.

"Rena emphasized that that people who are living their purpose and values enjoy life and are successful at what they do," he continued. "That was the key. I had to first discover, or actually rediscover, what was important to me and then start 'walking the talk' on my purpose and values.

"I am now practicing what I would call values-based leadership!"

"Wow!" replied Charlie. "But what does that mean? Did you come up with a definition of values-based leadership?"

"Yes I did, or actually the group at MMS deserves much of the credit. To us, values-based leaders are those whose decisions and actions are guided by an integrated set of values that jointly enhance human dignity and organization success."

"It sounds great! But you are going to have to explain that a bit more to a grizzled old veteran like myself."

THE DEFINITION OF VALUES-BASED LEADERSHIP

Values-based leaders are those whose decisions and actions are guided by an integrated set of values that jointly enhance human dignity and organization success.

"I would be happy to explain it more. To begin with, I thought we needed a term to identify the approach to leadership that I am using, and that we have adopted at MMS. I like the definition because it incorporates the two important components of leadership," Dave continued.

"The first component, the part of 'enhancing human dignity,' is a group of values that I have called character values. These are values such as integrity, respect, fair treatment, and development of others. That is the human dignity part. Those values develop trust and loyalty and commitment from the people you work with, as well as the development of skills and competency.

"You simply can't be a successful leader if people don't trust you or respect you, and the trust, respect, and commitment have to be earned. The only way to earn them is by exhibiting these character values.

"The second component, enhancing organization success, provides the sense of direction and focus. Having character values is great, and essential for leadership, but a leader also needs to provide a sense of direction and focus and community. That's the second group of values.

"As I said before, both sets of values are critical for leadership success. You need to have character to be a successful leader, but you also have to provide a vision and you have to build community."

"Let me show you how I think they fit together," Dave continued. With that he asked Charlie for a piece of paper, and on it he drew 2 × 2 model that Dar had designed.

He explained each of the four quadrants, and the type of people that fit into each quadrant.

When he came to the upper right-hand quadrant, the quadrant of the true value-based leaders, he said, "This is the square in which you find the true leaders—strong on character and strong on leading. Actually, Charlie, you are one of my poster boys for this square. I thought you were one of the most honest and decent people I ever worked for, and we always knew where we needed to go and how we would know if we were on target."

"Well, thank you for the kind words. And as to your model, I really like it!" Charlie exclaimed. "In fact, it fits a lot of my thinking about leadership. But I never thought of how to put it together so that I could explain it to anyone. I think you did it!"

"I also thought a lot of why the values-based approach is so important. Why focus on values? Why not focus on something else?" Dave continued, "Do you what to hear my thinking about that?"

"Keep going," answered Charlie, "I am really learning a lot about leadership."

"Well, we just wrote a preamble to our statement on values-based leadership, which is sort of a summary of our beliefs about this leadership approach. I know it by heart, so let me give you a quick summary. There are seven important points that underlie the values-based approach:

1. Values are the foundation of leadership. That is because values are very general and apply to many different situations. They may not tell you exactly what to do in a specific situation, but they give you some general guidelines on the criteria you should use to make your decision. For example, our values approach didn't tell us exactly what to do when we terminated a couple of Red's key people, but they served as important guidelines for making the decision.

2. It is those people who have a strong personal values base who have made and will make important (positive) contributions to their families, organizations, and the world.

3. Values and leadership come from inside the individual. Thus, if you want to make an impact, it is critical that you understand who you are and what you believe.

4. Values-based leadership includes both processes and outcomes. An elementary school teacher not only should treat each student with dignity, but also has the responsibility for making sure that students are learning in accordance with standards and potential.

5. Organizations can and do espouse values. Values become the basis for how organizations operate and are the foundation of their culture. The values are expressed in the policies and procedures, in leadership behavior, and a variety of little ways. Strong values organizations are more successful in the long term than are weak values organizations.

6. Values-based leaders create values-based organizations, groups, teams, families, and communities. By the standards they set, the decisions they make, the behaviors they exhibit, and the philosophy they espouse, values-based leaders have a significant influence on the behaviors of others and the workings of organizations.

7. People are most energized, motivated, and satisfied when their values and the values of the organization they are part of are in sync. In that instance, they are living out their purpose and values.

"That's it!" he concluded. "That is our preamble to our statement on values-based leadership."

"Wow! I am overwhelmed! And very impressed!" Charlie exclaimed. "But I do have a question regarding values-based organizations and MMS. You said values-based leaders create values-based organizations. How do you do that?"

"Good question! I am not exactly sure, but I can tell you what happened at MMS. Right after I finished developing my purpose and values with Rena, I told the executive team about my coaching sessions and how I discovered my values, and they responded very positively. Some of them developed their own list of personal values, and at their suggestion we are in the process of developing a leadership values statement for the company that we will be asking all employees to adhere to. In fact, we will be using the company values statement as a basis for hiring new people, as well as for the annual performance reviews and promotions."

"That brings up another question," Charlie said. "If the leader develops a set of personal leadership values, and the company or organization develops its own set of values that its leaders must follow, wouldn't that lead to confusion?"

"No, on the contrary, I think it would lead to clarification rather than confusion! When I was talking to Rena, I told her about my first job after college and how much I hated it and how it soured me on the business world—I may have told you about it at some point, too. I didn't really know it at the time but this job was a classic clash of values. I had one set of values and the group I was working for had another.

"It really would have been very helpful to me if I had clarified my purpose and values before I began that job. I would have known what my values were and quickly understood that the organization was not a good fit for me and could have moved on.

"That is why I think people should first define their purpose and values. Then, when they come into an organization they will know if the organization is compatible with their values. If it is a fit, great! If it is not a fit, they have the choice of changing the organization values or looking for an organization with a better fit.

"Let me put it another way. Values-based leaders know who they are, what they believe in, and what they want to accomplish in life."

"Wow," said Charlie, "you and Rena really connected. I know she did some values coaching at Kron, but I wasn't really sure what it was all about. Maybe I should have gone to one of her sessions."

"Actually, we hired Rena to facilitate a couple of workshops for the employees at MMS," Dave said. "The workshops are called Becoming a Values-Based Leader, and what she does is go through the steps that she put me through in our coaching sessions, including identifying the people who had an influence on your life, and identifying one's life values. The workshops are open to anyone at MMS, and are strictly voluntary, but they are usually filled to capacity. "

"I am really impressed," said Charlie. "Things are really moving at MMS. But what about Redbeard the Pirate? Wasn't he one of the reasons you were thinking of leaving MMS? What does he think about this values stuff?"

"Oh, yes, my old problem Red Morgan." Dave said, "Actually, Red retired about six weeks ago. He said that the business was changing too fast for him. He said we were too hung up on values and things like that, and that we really didn't understand how to build sales. So, he said goodbye, and we did give him a nice retirement party.

"And the new person Anita put in charge of the West Coast is doing great. She quickly replaced a couple of the people on Red's sales team—sort of cleaned house. But in spite of the changes, or maybe because of the changes, sales seem to be growing nicely in the territory."

"And you have no interest in going back to Kron, I assume?" Charlie asked.

"No way, I am having too much fun at MMS! Why would I want to go back to Kron and miss all the fun?" Dave said laughingly, and with a smile on his face told Charlie, "And I hate to cut this discussion short, but Nancy and I are going to have to take our leave. We promised the kids we would take them shopping for Halloween pumpkins later today. Again, thanks for your help, and thanks so much for inviting us today."

They had reached the patio again and Dave and Nancy said their goodbyes to the Schaefers. As they walked to Dave's car Charlie told Dave how pleased he was that things are working out at MMS and that Dave's "leadership crisis" was over.

"I'm intrigued by this values-based leadership approach, and how you are putting it together," he said. "Do you think it would work for an old part-time consultant like me?"

"You would love it," replied Dave, "it is right up your alley. In fact, I will give Rena your email address and ask her to include you in the next session she does for us."

"Aren't you afraid that I might steal your values?" Charlie said, laughing.

"Nope," Dave responded. "You can't steal values. Values are free to everyone. The tough part is walking the walk. That's what makes the difference in leadership. But I am sure that Rena will find you an A+ student in that respect."

And with that the Dave gave Charlie a hug, and he and Nancy headed home.

APPENDIX

Steps and Exercises for Becoming a Values-Based Leader

Listed below are the steps and exercises that Dave used in his quest to become a Values-Based Leader. As noted in the story of his work with Rena, the process takes several weeks. This allows sufficient time for reflection on each step. For example, in the first step you are asked to identify the four or five people who most significantly impacted your life. Usually this takes some time and thought, and often one comes up with people that would not be obvious if one had made quick judgments.

Likewise, deciding one's life purpose usually takes time and reflection. This is not a question most people have thought about, however, it gets at the heart of who you are. Moreover, one's purpose and values often change over time. For example, the value of family, or family as part of one's purpose, often becomes more prominent as one grows older.

So, the message here is take your time, write out each exercise, and please change your answers as you have new insights. Enjoy your journey!

Step #1:

Who were (are) the important people in your life?

Who were (are) the four or five people who most significantly impacted your life? Briefly describe each. Why were they important in your life? What did you learn from them that you would like to emulate?

Step #2:

What is your purpose in life?

What is your life purpose? What would you like to accomplish in your life? Why would it be important (to you) to accomplish that?

Step #3:

What are your life values?

What are your five or six most important life values? These are the values that you would use to guide your life

How would you "walk the talk" on each of these values? That is, if you were living these values to the fullest, what would we see you doing?

Step #4:

What is leadership?

What is your definition of effective leadership? What are some of the most important responsibilities of a leader? What do effective leaders do that distinguishes them from leaders that are not effective?

Step #5:

What are your leadership values?

What do you see as the most important values of leadership? These have to be your values, not something you read in a book.

If you were practicing these values to their fullest, what would we see you doing? That is, how would a person "walk the talk" on the values you have chosen? How will you "walk the talk" on your values? How will you live your values at home and at work?

Step #6:

Communicating your values

How would you communicate your life values, and/or your leadership values, to your associates? How will they know what you stand for, and what they can expect from you?

Step #7:

Assuming that you could (and want to) create a values-based work unit, or a values-based organization, how would you go about doing this. What are the steps in the process? Who will be involved? What outcome would you hope for?